By Oriana Fallaci

Oriana Fallaci

The FORCE
of
REASON

(La FORZA della RAGIONE)

Rizzoli
International

Published by Rizzoli International Publications, Inc.
300 Park Avenue South
New York, NY 10010
www.rizzoliusa.com

Library of Congress Catalog Control Number: 2005935245

ISBN-10 0-8478-2753-4

ISBN-13 978-0-8478-2753-4

Original Title: **La Forza della Ragione**

Printed in Italy
February 2006

2006 2007 2008 2009 2010 / 10 9 8 7 6 5 4 3 2 1

TO THE ENGLISH-SPEAKING READER

As I did for "The Rage and the Pride"
when I published it in the United States
in September 2002,
I take upon myself the responsibility
for this translation.
Although it has been somewhat revised,
it may contain what certain critics define
as "the oddities of Fallaci's English".
Meaning, a punctuation and a lexical choice
and above all a sentence structure
which reflects or repeats my way
of writing in Italian. My language.
Though admitting those possible oddities,
I choose to offer the text as it is because,
given the importance of what I speak about,
and given the tragic grievousness of what I say,
I must bear the full burden
of every word I publish under my name
in this language I love as much as my own.

Oriana Fallaci

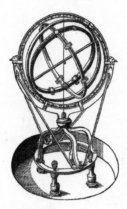

«They are flooding all over
the city now buried
into torpor and sleep and wine,
the invaders. And meanwhile,
through its open gates,
others irrupt to join
their henchmen's platoons».

(Virgil, *The Aeneid.* The burning of Troy)

PROLOGUE

*A sharp and mordant man, an autho-
rity in difficult Sciences and by cultured youths
much beloved, by Pope John himself admired and
esteemed but by envious enemies much hated, in
1327 Messer Francesco da Ascoli better known as
Mastro Cecco wrote an essay which he called
«The Armillary Sphere». A controversial book
where, speaking of his times, he argued things as
displeasing to the Inquisition as dear to the wise
people and to the wise pupils of the Philosophical
School he kept in Florence. And since this did not
please the Duke of Calabria who besides being
Lord of the City was the firstborn of Robert d'An-
giò king of Naples, since this pleased even less his
First Minister who besides being Friar Conven-
tual was the Bishop of Aversa, the culprit was arrested. He was taken to the Florentine gaol of the
Holy Office and given over to a certain Fra' Accursio of the Order of Preachers, by Apostolic ap-*

9

pointment Grand Inquisitor in the Province of Tuscany. By persons who would not and should not and could not understand its arguments, «The Armillary Sphere» was thus scrutinized and judged as an impious, profane, indecent, abject publication. A book incompatible with the orthodox faith, composed on the Devil's suggestion, infected by the most pernicious heresy. And as an iniquitous sorcerer for several months Mastro Cecco was subjected to the most rigorous tortures plus goaded to acknowledge his Faults and disavow his Errors. But in vain. To every torture he replied that it was not a matter of fault or error, that he had said and written and taught those things because they were true. And because he believed in them.

It was so that on the 20 day of September 1328 they took him to the Church of Santa Croce, for the occasion decked out in black. They placed him upon a high stage especially assembled and in the presence of an innumerable mob, innumerable authorities, innumerable doctors and councillors of the Holy Office they read him the compendium of the trial. They listed all the impieties of the controversial essay and again they asked him if he wished to repent, to disavow, to save his life in extremis. But again he refused. Again he replied that he had said and written and taught

those things because they were true, because he
believed in them. It was so that Fra' Accursio declared him a recidivist, an impenitent heretic, a
ruin for himself and the others, an evil plant to be
extirpated. Then, after invoking the grace of God
and of the Holy Spirit, he condemned him to be
burned alive together with his wicked book and
all the blameworthy writings he had published.
He also ordained that within fifteen days any
copy in possession of the citizens be brought to
him forthwith for destruction. He also added that
whosoever held or concealed them would be
struck by excommunication and corporal and spiritual and pecuniary punishment. Then he had
the culprit brought down from the stage. He had
him dressed in the Sanbenito, which was a cruel
sackcloth with painted devils. He made him ridiculous by placing on his head a farcical dunce's
mitre and by taking off his shoes. In such appea-
rance he handed him over to Messer Jacopo da
Brescia, executor of Justice in Tuscany and vicar
of the Inquisition's Secular Arm.

The sentence was carried out after the procession which preceded every execution, and took
place outside the Gate of the Cross where a tall
stake with a great quantity of firewood had been
erected. Upon the firewood, all the copies of «The
Armillary Sphere» and the other volumes which

11

had been confiscated. With supreme intrepidity and contemptuously deploring the ignorance, the bigotry, the hypocrisy, the lack of Reason in which his epoch lived, Mastro Cecco let himself be bound to the stake. And in a short time he burnt. Like paper he turned to ashes along with his books. But his thought remained.

Author's note. I reconstructed this account from the chronicles of the *Inquisizione in Toscana*: the book compiled by abbot Modesto Rastrelli and printed in 1782 by Anton Giuseppe Pagani, publisher in Florence. The language wants to echo the style of the abbot who used terms in fashion at the times of Mastro Cecco and told things paradoxically valid also today. Besides, also today's events are in substance the same.

As to the Armillary Sphere, we well know that it was the astronomic instrument (presumedly conceived by Archimedes) once employed to measure the apparent motions of the Sun and composed by metal circles crossing each other. (As the old drawing on the page preceding this prologue shows).

More than three years have elapsed since the day when, like a Cassandra talking to the wind, I published *The Rage and the Pride*. That scream of pain which the Fra' Accursios defined as impious, profane, indecent, abject, a book opposite to orthodox faith, an iniquity written on the Devil's suggestion and infected by the most pernicious heresy. That J'accuse which has engorged me as *The Armillary Sphere* had engorged Mastro Cecco, like me guilty of saying that the Earth is round, like me culpable of printing the truth that ignorance and bigotry and hypocrisy and lack of Reason never want to hear. Oh, in my case the thugs of today's Holy Office (the secular one) do not recur to the body of excruciations they used for Mastro Cecco in 1327 and 1328. Although I too have been pilloried, exposed to public outrage, Messer Jacopo da Brescia has not burnt me alive on the stake (or not yet) together with the wicked book and my other blameworthy writings. Today's (I mean secular) Inquisition is shrewd, you see. It fights death penalty and instead of the body it tortures the soul, instead of the pincers or the ropes or the axes it uses blood-less tools: newspapers, radio, television, journalists, politicians, unsuccessful academics, movie starlets. Instead of the jails controlled by the Holy Office it uses stadiums, squares, marches which taking advantage of freedom kill freedom. Instead of cowls (but often you see the cowls too) it uses djellabahs and chadors and the tracksuits of the rainbow-flaggers who call themselves «pacifists», or the blue suits and the red ties of their puppet-masters. (Members of the Parliament, writers, trade-union ringleaders, reporters, bankers, prelates. The new valets of the Holy Office, in short, the Fra' Accursios who serve a power smuggled as anti-Power). In other words, it has changed its face. But its essence is unaltered. And if you write that the Earth is round, you become an outlaw right away. A heretic to be burned, a Mastro Cecco.

I may seem ungrateful, in saying these things, I know. And in a way I am. The inferno poured on my *Armillary Sphere*, in fact, has also brought me a great deal of love. Of respect, of gratitude, of love. In France, for instance, a website set up with the address «thankyouoriana» has collected in one year 56.000 messages of thanks. Some of them, sent from countries where *The Rage and the Pride* had not been translated. From Bosnia, from Morocco, Nigeria, Iran. (And there

14

the thankyouorianas were signed by Muslim women living under the yoke of the Sharia, needless to say). In Moscow the manager of a chemical factory has improvised an underhand translation that he reads to his workers as if it were the Bible. In America some newspapers have dedicated to that book praises which sound almost embarassing. The *New York Post*, to give an example, has called me «the exception in a time where honesty and moral clarity are no longer considered precious virtues». It has also published the letter of a Miami reader who says: «Fallaci's book reminds me of Winston Churchill's *Step by Step*, the appeal with which Churchill reprimanded Europe for its inertia in front of Hitler and Mussolini». (Also the appeal, I underline, for which the «pacifists» of the Forties called him a warmonger). And a New York reader has added: «It seems that the only articulate intellectual produced by Europe since Winston Churchill's famous Iron Curtain-speech is Oriana Fallaci. Her judgement of radical Islam is unimpeachable». As for the affectionate letters sent me from France, Germany, Spain, Holland, Hungary and Scandinavia, I have lost the count. Those from Italy fill many boxes and one that I'll never forget says: «Thank you, Fallaci, for teaching me to think what I did not know I was thinking». Another one says:

«Two years ago I allowed myself to be swayed by the lynching that the cicadas had unchained against you. So I too yelled against you. But I was wrong. The facts have proved and prove that you were right, you are right, and now I burn like you with rage and pride». But this does not console me. Or not as much as it should. Because when I think of the people who think as I do the horizon broadens, and the victims of bigotry or hypocrisy or lack of Reason increase. I find out that Fra' Accursism has become a way of life, a way of judging which blooms particularly in the countries ruled by democracy. For example in France, in England, in Germany, in Spain, in Italy where in every home, every office, every school, every factory, every place of work or study you find a Mastro Cecco or a Mastra Cecca who in one way or another undergoes the abuses I have undergone during the last two years.

What abuses? Well, it gives me nausea to list them all. Worse: it risks to turn the problem into a personal matter. But if I don't mention them, those who don't know won't understand. So, here they are. Death threats, to start with. Bellowed or whispered, phoned or handwritten or printed. The printed ones, in libellous publications spread out in the Islamic communities. Illiterate booklets which even dare defaming the memory of my beloved father and urge the Muslims to kill me in the name of the Koran. (To be precise, in the name of four Surahs according to which before being executed as an infidel-bitch I should be stripped and exposed to unspeakable abuses). Repulsive articles which defame another dead man whom I beloved, my companion Alekos Panagulis. Withering vulgarities published with equal satisfaction by newspapers of the Left and the Right. «Or-Hyena Fallaci», for instance. «Taliban Fallaci», «Fuck-you-Fallaci». (The Fuck-you-Fallaci appeared in an Extreme Left newspaper in letters big enough to cover the whole page). And obscenities written on the street walls or the placards of the rainbow-flaggers who call themselves pacifists. («Oriana whore»). Banners inviting me to disintegrate on the next shuttle which will blow up. Television conductors who during their show draw enormous moustaches on my photos. (Usually, photos as large as two yards). And who while doing so announce that in the next show they will repeat the bravado. Politicians (mainly Communists or ex-Communists) who see in my ideas the sign of a neurological disorder caused by advancing age. And who in a classic Bolshevik style suggest I be shut up inside a psychiatric clinic. Female comedians who make fun of me wearing a helmet like the one I used in Vietnam. Who call me warmonger like Churchill. Who ridiculize my illness with gags. («I hope you get a cancer!» yells a supporting actor to the comedian impersonating Fallaci with the helmet. So she answers: «I already have it». And the audience laughs). That particular gag took place also when in Florence the «pacifists» made their half a million people march with the intention of smearing indelible paint on the monuments, but I induced the authorities to deny them access to the Historical Center. And it was precisely on such an occasion, six hundred seventy four years after the burning of Mastro Cecco, that Florence rang with the scream «Burn-her-books, make-a-bonfire-with-her-books». It was precisely on such an occasion that outside the basilica of Santa Croce, in the very churchyard where Fra'Accursio had pronounced the death sentence of Mastro Cecco, I was exposed to public outrage. And do you know who instigated the crowd to yell insults against me? A buffoon bestowed with the Nobel Prize and kindly received in the United States, a Red Fascist who in the Second World War had been a Black Fascist. Meaning, an ally of Hitler. But here I need to digress for a moment on the world's most betrayed, most insulted, most violated word. The word «peace». So let me open a parenthesis.

* * *

    Parenthesis. Dear pacifists, (but given your belligerancy and bellicosity, I should use your term «war-mongers»), what do you mean when you speak of peace? A Utopian world where people love each other the way Jesus preached though Jesus was not much of a pacifist? «Think not that I am come to bring peace on earth» he said. «I came not to bring peace, I came to bring a sword. I came to separate the son from the father, the daughter from the mother, the daughter in law from the mother in law». (The Gospel according to St. Matthew, Chapter 10, verses 34-35). And what do you mean when you speak of war? Only the war which is waged with tanks, artillery, airplanes, helicopters etcetera? Then, what about the war which is waged with the suicide-bombers' explosives, with the kamikazes who kill even three thousand people at a time? This question concerns also the pacifists of the Catholic Church. A Church which on such matter is the first one to use double standards. Which, apart from burning heretics, for centuries has sullied our world with its wars. Which for centuries prospered on the warrior Popes. Which with its crocodile tears and its Peace-on-Earth-encyclicals now expects to restore a virginity that not even all the Hollywood's plastic surgeons could re-establish. But it concerns especially the hypocrites who never wave their rainbow flags to condemn the terrorists who wage war with suicide bombs or the remote-controlled bombs or the imams who preach the war in their mosques. Or the wind-bags who, not realizing it because in spite of their doctorates are ignorant to boot, plagiarize the senselessness published in 1795 by Immanuel Kant.

In 1795 Kant published an essay entitled *Perpetual Peace*. A demagogical essay where, with no regard for the history of this planet and the events taking place under his own eyes, he said that wars were started exclusively by monarchies. Ergo, only republics could bring peace. He said it when the Republican France, the France of the French Revolution, the France which had guillotined Louis XVI and Marie Antoinette and abolished the monarchy, was fighting the monarchies of Austria and Prussia in a war that the same revolutionaries had declared three years earlier. When in the Vendée they conducted a fratricidal war against the Catholics and the monarchists. (Mostly peasants and woodcutters). When in Paris the man of the slogan Liberté-Egalité-Fraternité prepared himself to bring war inside all the corners of Europe plus Egypt and Russia. That is, when the super-republican Napoleon Bonaparte made his debut as a general and on behalf of the Directory quenched with rivers of blood the monarchist insurrection. For Christsake, it is since then that opportunists mimic the one-way pacifism of Immanuel Kant and resort to war with brazen-faced impudence. They do it in the name of humanity, of course. And, more than often, waving a revolutionary flag. Because also a revolution is a war, dear big-mouths. A civil war, a carnage identical to the carnage of an average war. Just to stay in our recent times, think again of the French Revolution and of its abominations. Or of the Russian Revolution and the Chinese Revolution and of their atrocities. Or think of the Spanish Civil War, think of the Vietnam war, (which was a civil war in every sense and whoever denies it is a moron), think of the war in Cambodia which was even worse. Think of the bloodbaths in which African countries have destructed and still destruct themselves since the end of colonialism. And think of the civil war (morally a civil war) which a good number of westerners are fighting against the West. Then read Plato.

Plato says that war exists and will always exist because it comes from human passions. He says that there is no getting away from it because it belongs to human nature, to our anger and arrogance, our need to assert and exert dominance or supremacy. Which is certainly true. If you ponder a little, you conclude that every deed of ours is an act of war. Each of our actions is a form of war waged against someone or something. Professional and political rivalry, for instance, are a form of war. Elections are a form of war. Competition in all of its facets is a form of war. And certain sports are full-blown war. Including soccer which I have never liked because the sight of twenty-two guys stealing a ball from each other, kicking and kneeing each other, disturbs me deeply. And don't talk to me about boxing or wrestling. The spectacle of two men harming each other, smashing each other's nose and mouth, dislocating each other's arms and legs, twisting each other's necks, horrifies me. However, Plato is wrong when he says that war comes from human passions, that only man makes war. When a lion pursues a gazelle, sinks its teeth in its throat and rips its body to pieces, it commits an act of war. When a bird swoops down on a worm, grabs it in its beak and swallows it alive, it commits an act of war. When a fish eats another fish, an insect eats another insect, a gamete pursues another gamete, they commit an act of war. When weeds invade a cornfield, the same. Even an ivy that wraps itself around a tree commits an act of war. War is not a curse which characterizes human nature: it is a curse which characterizes Life. There is no way to avoid war because war is a part of Life. Repulsive, hideous? Of course. So hideous that my atheism stems mainly from it. That is, from my refusal to accept the idea of a Creator who invented a world where Life kills Life, where Life eats Life. A world where in order to survive one has to kill and eat other living beings. Be they chickens or clams or tomatoes. If such an existence had been conceived by a Creator, I say, that Creator would be a very nasty one indeed.

I don't either believe in the masochism of turning the other cheek, nevertheless. And if I am invaded by weeds, suffocated by ivy, poisoned by an insect, bitten by a dog, attacked by a human being, I fight. I make war, I fight. I do so with a weapon which does not spread blood, agree. The weapon of ideas expressed through the written word, not through death. But should that weapon not be enough, I would be ready to make war with something more. Like I did as a young girl when my country was invaded by weeds, suffocated by ivy, poisoned by insects, bitten by dogs, subdued by the enemy. And no jester bawling at me in a square, no jackass smearing my photo on TV, no vicious comedienne deriding my deadly illness is going to stop me. No march of louts waving disgusting placards is going to intimidate me, to shut me up. No son of Allah calling out to punish-the-infidel-bitch in the name of the Koran is going to frighten me or tire me out. Even if I am in the evening of my life and I no longer have the physical energy of youth. Because my war is right. Legitimate, dutiful, right. And it is not true that all wars are wrong. Sometimes they are right. Legitimate, dutiful, right.

Parenthesis closed.

*   *   *

The list of abuses (for pity's sake or rather for my country's sake I shall not dwell on those perpetrated by the deities of the Constitutional Olympus who in public events lower themselves by using my surname as a derogatory noun or adjective. Fallacy, fallacious, and so on) also includes the trial celebrated against me in Paris. A trial promoted for religious racism, xenophobia, blasphemy, instigation to hatred of Islam. A trial undertaken, I still cannot believe it, with the contribution of the leftist Jewish association «Licra». (Apparently unmindful of the manifesto I had just written against the resurgence of anti-Semitism in Europe). It also includes the unforgivable obscenity which blackened the name of the country so dear to the tyrants who loose their throne and need its banks. I mean Switzerland. That Switzerland where the sons of Allah are now more numerous and more arrogant than at Mecca. And where in 1995 the Article 261b of the Criminal Code was written for their benefit. (The Article which allows a Muslim immigrant to win any ideological or private lawsuit by invoking religious racism and racial discrimination. «He-didn't-chase-me-because-I'm-a-thief-but-because-I'm-a-Muslim»). Quoting the Article 261b, in fact, through the Swiss Embassy in Rome in November 2002 the Berne Federal Office of Justice dared to ask the Italian government to extradite me or to open legal proceedings against me for the content of *The Rage and the Pride*. Proceedings requested by Muslim groups like the Islamic Center of Berne, the Somali Association of Geneva, the SOS Racism of Lausanne, and Islamic immigrants living in the town of Neuchâtel. Counts of indictment, my «racist behaviour» and my judgements on Islam. Judgements, they said, sustained by ideas which «endanger public peace and generate hate among those who believe in the clash of civilization».

The request was flatly denied by the Italian Minister of Justice, Roberto Castelli, who reminded his Swiss counterpart that the Italian Constitution guarantees the right to express any thought both in speech and in writing. As a consequence, asking to prosecute a citizen for his or her ideas was an insult to a fundamental principle of the Italian Constitution and to the dignity of the Italian State. Yet various members of the Left expressed the hope that I would be tried in Switzerland all the same and, given the fact that Switzerland has the nasty habit of prosecuting in the absence plus without the knowledge of the accused, I dont't know if in Geneva or Berne or Zurich or Lausanne I have been convicted or not. The Article 261b has already done so many victims. One is the Animal Rights activist Erwin Kessler who like Brigitte Bardot cannot abide the Muslims practice to butcher the lambs like Dracula, that is, slowly drawing their blood. For criticizing it, he got two months in prison and no suspension of sentence. Another one is the 80-year old historian Gaston Armand Amaudruz who used to print a revisionist monthly (revising history, refusing its official version, is by now forbidden) and because of that was sentenced by the Court of Lausanne to one year in prison plus a heavy fine. Another one is the French historian Robert Faurisson who in 2001 was prosecuted by the Court of Fribourg and sentenced to a month's imprisonment. The reason, an article he had published in France then given to a Swiss magazine. (Despite his late age, he too was denied suspension of sentence). Anyway Switzerland is not the only country where I risk to end behind bars. Most of Europe, in fact, has become for me a possible threat. Do you know why? Because the European Union exercises a perversion called European Arrest Warrant. And the European Arrest Warrant is a mandate which not only permits any European country to arrest and keep in jail any citizen belonging to the Union: it is an abuse which permits to impose the extradition from his or her own homeland.

Conceived to obstruct the flights of criminals moving from country to country, until September 11 this mandate should have covered crimes such as terrorism, murder, kidnapping, drug-trafficking, child prostitution, paedophilia, illegal traffic of arms and nuclear or radioactive material. But eight days after September 11 the leftist European Commission slipped into it also the crimes of racism, xenophobia, blasphemy and racial discrimination. So, when the European Arrest Warrant will be endorsed by the countries which have not endorsed it as yet, any free mind of the continent will risk to become an international Mastro Cecco. A heretic who at any time and in any place can be extradited in handcuffs from his or her homeland because of some accusation presented by a Muslim. Extradited and (I use the terms of the mandate itself) held «in preventive custody for at least four months». Extradited and prosecuted under laws which in Europe are applied with the same double standards used for the word Peace. And be sure: any pretext will do. Because if you speak your mind on the Vatican, on the Catholic Church, on the Pope, on the Virgin Mary or Jesus or the Saints, nobody touches your «right of thought and expression». But if you do the same with Islam, the Koran, the Prophet Mohammed, some son of Allah, you are called a xenophobic blasphemer who has committed an act of racial discrimination. If you kick the ass of a Chinese or an Eskimo or a Norwegian who has hissed at you an obscenity, nothing happens. On the contrary, you get a «Well done, good for you». But if under the same circumstances you kick the ass of an Algerian or a Moroccan or a Nigerian or a Sudanese, you get lynched. If you yell anti-American slogans, if you call the Americans «murderers» or «ruffians» or «enemies of humankind», if you burn their flags, if you stick swastikas on photographs of their presidents, nothing happens. On the contrary, such aggression is considered an act of virtue. But if you say and do the identical thing against Islam, you end up on the stake. The same if you think that western civilization is the most advanced one that this planet has ever produced.

The same if you define it as «superior». But if you are a son of Allah and say that Islam has always been a superior civilization, a Ray of Light, and if according to the Koran you add that Christians stink like goats and pigs and camels and monkeys together, nobody touches you. Nobody prosecutes you. Nobody convicts you.

Besides, this happens also inside the pro-Islamic UN. This UN about which the fools and the hypocrites always speak in a reverent way, to which they refer as if it were a fair and honest and impartial mother. «Take-it-to-the-UN». «Bring-in-the-UN». «Let-the-UN-decide». This UN which in total contempt of the Universal Declaration of Human Rights (a document that Muslim countries have never accepted to sign up) in 1977 accepted to recognize the «Declaration of Human Rights in Islam». Meaning, a declaration which states: «All the following rights are subject to the Islamic Law, to the Sharia. In Islamic countries the Sharia is the only source of reference with regard to human rights». This UN whose ambiguous Commission on Human Rights has hosted a seminar in 1997 financed by the Islamic Conference and named «Islamic Perspectives on the Universal Declaration of Human Rights». Moreover, a seminar which asked «to extend all over the world the Islamic perspectives on human rights» and to remind «the contribution given by Islam in laying their foundations». By the way, «rights thanks to which Islam has always guided the world and uprooted it from darkness, enlightened it as well cleared that all human beings must submit to Allah as the Koran demands»... This UN which in 1999 censured the Brazilian Maurice Glèlè Ahanhanzo, then Special Relator, for devoting twenty-five pages of his report to the anti-Semitism spread in the Arab countries. This UN where the Pakistani Ambassador dares to say (unopposed) that «the first Charter of Human Rights is the Koran and the first Declaration of Human Rights was pronounced by Mohammed in Medina»... This UN which brazenly protects the Islamic fundamentalist dictatorship in Sudan and has never allowed John Garang (the Christian leader of the Sudanese Liberation Movement) to open his mouth before its committees or its Assembly... This UN which along with the ineffable European Union has invented the crimes of «Islamophobia» and «defamation of Islam». In fact there too I have a Fra' Accursio.

Who is my Fra' Accursio at the UN? Well, it is the Senegalese Doudou Diène, one-time bigshot in the formerly pro-Soviet UNESCO. In 2002 he was appointed Special Relator, I mean, he succeeded the removed Maurice Glèlè Ahanhanzo, and guess what his credentials were: the reports on the cases of islamophobia which «since September 11 were afflicting the Muslims of America and Europe». According to him, the two continents where «Muslim women and elderly people and children are victims of continuous physical and verbal attacks and abuses coming from the non-Muslims. So they continuously live in terror». On these «attacks and abuses» he has also written another report asking the Commission on Human Rights to hold a Moral Trial in Geneva. And guess who are this time the culprits to be judged, the heretics to be burnt on the stake: the American leaders of the Evangelical Churches who fight Islamic slavery in Sudan. I mean the sixty intellectuals who led by Samuel Huntington signed the open letter «What We Are Fighting For». With them, the Baptist minister Jerry Falwell who defends the Ten Commandments and Mr. Pat Robertson who founded the Christian Broadcasting Network. In Europe, «the intellectuals who oppose immigration and reject the cultural pluralism, put Islam on trial, maintain that Islam is incompatible with secularism. And who, in doing so, *light up the international disorder*». Leading the conspiracy, the turpitude, Oriana Fallaci and two Frenchmen: author Pierre Manent and scholar Alain Finkielkraut. Fallaci because she writes what she writes. Manent because he says to be against the dialogue with Islam and asks the Muslims to go back home. Finkielkraut because he has defended my book *The Rage and the Pride* with the following statement: «Far from being racist, Fallaci compels us to look reality in the face, breaks taboos, and fearlessly exercises freedom». But this is only a tiny part of the auto-da-fé unleashed by the one-time bigshot of the formerly pro-Soviet UNESCO Doudou Diène. From Geneva, in fact, Doudou has already demanded the UN to «devise a cultural strategy and extirpate the ideologies which defame Islam. Plus, to promote a worldwide conference with the authority of controlling how-History-is-written-or-rather-taught-in-the-West».

* * *

Therefore the rage that shook me up more than three years ago, when I wrote *The Rage and the Pride*, has not abated. On the contrary, it has doubled. The pride that more than three years ago stiffened me like a sword has not withered. On the contrary, it has reinforced. And when a Fra' Accursio asks me if I regret something of what I wrote, if in what I wrote there is something I wish to abjure, I answer: «Far from it, Holy Excellency.

My only regret is to have said less than I should. To have called simply "cicadas" those that today I call collaborationists, traitors». Then I add that the rage and the pride have married each other and produced a sturdy son: the disdain. And disdain has intensified my cogitation, reinvigorated my reason. Reason has brought into focus the truths that feelings had not focused and that now I can express without half-measures, without restraints. For instance, by asking: what kind of democracy is a democracy that forbids dissent, that punishes it, that turns it into a crime? What kind of democracy is a democracy that instead of listening to its children silences them, hands them to the enemy, abandons them to abuse and bullying? What kind of democracy is a democracy that favours theocracy, that re-establishes heresy, that tortures and burns the free minds on the stake? What kind of democracy is a democracy where the minority counts for more than the majority and where, counting for more than the majority, it swaggers and blackmails?!? A non-democracy, I say. A deceit, a lie. And what kind of freedom is a freedom which prevents us from thinking, from speaking, from going against the wind, from rebelling, from opposing those who invade us and muzzle us? What kind of freedom is a freedom that makes citizens live in the fear of being prosecuted and convicted as criminals? What kind of freedom is a freedom that along with the thought wants to censor the feelings, to decide whom I must love and whom I must hate, so that if I hate Americans I go to Heaven and if I hate Muslims I go to Hell? A non-freedom, I say. A mockery, a farce.

With disdain and in the name of Reason, then, I resume the discourse that more than three years ago I ended with the words enough-stop-enough. With disdain and in the name of Reason I emulate Mastro Cecco, I make myself a recidivist, I publish my second *The Armillary Sphere*. While Troy burns. While Europe becomes more and more a province of Islam, a colony of Islam. And my country an outpost of that province, a stronghold of that colony.

CHAPTER 1

I don't like to say that Troy is burning. That Europe is by now a province of Islam or rather a colony of Islam and Italy an outpost of that province, a stronghold of that colony. Saying this amounts to admitting that the Cassandras really do talk to the wind, that in spite of their screams of pain the blind remain blind, the deaf remain deaf, consciences reawoken soon relapse into sleep, and the Mastros Cecco die for nothing. But the truth is just this. From the Strait of Gibraltar to the fjords of Sørøy, from the cliffs of Dover to the beaches of Lampedusa, from the steppes of Volgograd to the valleys of the Loire and the hills of Tuscany, the fire is spreading. In each one of our cities there is a second city. A city superimposed and equal to the one that in the Seventies thousands and thousands of Palestinians set up in Beirut installing a State within the State. A government within the government. A Muslim city, a city ruled by the Koran. An Islamic expansionism's stage. The expansionism that no-one has ever managed to overcome. No-one. Not even the armies of Napoleon.

Because it is the only art in which the sons of Allah have always excelled, the art of invading and conquering and subjugating. Their most coveted prey has always been Europe, the Christian world, and shall we run a rapid eye over the History that Mr. Doudou would like to control or rather cancel?

* * *

It was in 635 AD, that is three years after Mohammed's death, that the armies of the Crescent Moon invaded Christian Syria and Christian Palestine. It was in 638 that they took Jerusalem and the Holy Sepulchre. It was in 640 that after conquering Persia and Armenia and Mesopotamia, present-day Iraq, they invaded Christian Egypt and overran Christian Maghreb. That is, the present Tunisia and Algeria and Morocco. It was in 668 that for the first time they attacked Constantinople and laid a siege that would last five years. It was in 711 that after crossing the Strait of Gibraltar they landed in the most Catholic Iberian Peninsula, took possession of Portugal and Spain where despite the Pelayos and the Cid Campeadors and the other warriors engaged in the Reconquest they remained for no less than eight centuries. And whoever believes in the myth of «peaceful coexistence that marked the relationships between the conquered and the conquerors» should reread the stories of the burned convents and monasteries, of the profaned churches, of the raped nuns, of the Christian or Jewish women abducted to be locked away in their harems. He should ponder on the crucifixions of Cordoba, the hangings of Granada, the beheadings of Toledo and Barcelona, of Seville and Zamora. (The beheadings of Seville, ordered by Mutamid: the king who used those severed heads, heads of Jews and Christians, to adorn his palace. The beheadings of Zamora, ordered by Almanzor: the vizier who was called the-patron-of-the-philosophers, the greatest leader Islamic Spain ever produced). Christ! Invoking the name of Jesus meant instant execution. Crucifixion, of course, or decapitation or hanging or impalement. Ringing a bell, the same. Wearing green, the colour exclusive to Islam, also. And when a Muslim passed by, every Jew and Christian was obliged to step aside. To bow. And mind to the Jew or the Christian who dared react to the insults of a Muslim. As for the much-flaunted detail that the infidel-dogs were not obliged to convert to Islam, not even encouraged to do so, do you know why they were not? Because those who converted to Islam did not pay taxes. Those who refused, on the contrary, did.

From Spain, in 721 AD, they passed into the no less Catholic France. Led by Abd al-Rahman, the Governor of Andalusia, they crossed the Pyrenees and took Narbonne. There they massacred the entire male population, enslaved all the women and children, then proceeded towards Carcassonne. From Carcassonne they went to Nîmes where they slaughtered nuns and friars. From Nîmes they went to Lyons and Dijon where they pillaged every single church... And do you know how long their advance in France lasted? Eleven years. In waves. In 731 a wave of three hundred and eighty thousand infantry and sixteen thousand cavalry reached Bordeaux which surrendered at once. Then from Bordeaux it moved to Poitiers, from Poiters it moved to Tours and, if in 732 Charles Martel had not won the battle of Poitiers-Tours, today the French too would dance the flamenco. In 827 they landed in Sicily, another target of their voraciousness. Massacring, beheading, impaling, crucifying as usual, they conquered Syracuse and Taormina then Messina and Palermo, and in three-quarters of a century (which was what it took to break the proud resistance of the Sicilians) they Islamized the island. They stayed for over two centuries, in Sicily: until they were cleared out by the Normans. But in 836 they landed at Brindisi. In 840, at Bari. And they Islamized Puglia too. In 841 they landed at Ancona. Then from the Adriatic they moved back to the Tyrrhenian Sea and in the summer of 846 landed at Ostia. They sacked it, they burned it, and moving upriver from the mouth of the Tiber they reached Rome. They laid siege to it and one night they burst in. They plundered the basilicas of St. Peter and St. Paul, sacked both, and to get rid of them Pope Sergius II had to stipulate an annual tribute of twenty-five thousand pieces of silver. To prevent further attacks, his successor Leo IV had to erect the Leonine Walls.

Having left Rome, though, they descended on Campania. They stayed there for seventy years destroying Montecassino and tormenting Salerno. A city where, at one time, they amused themselves by sacrificing a nun's virginity every night. Do you know where? On the cathedral's altar. In 898 they landed in Provence. To be precise, in present-day Saint-Tropez. They settled there, and in 911 crossed the Alps to enter Piedmont. They occupied Turin and Casale, set fire to all the churches and libraries, killed thousands of Christians, then went to Switzerland. Here they reached the Graubünden valley and the lake of Geneva. Then, put off by the snow, did an about-turn and returned to the warm climate of Provence. In 940 they occupied Toulon where they settled and... Today it's fashionable to beat our breast over the Crusades. To blame the West for the Crusades. To see the Crusades as an injustice committed to the detriment of the poor-innocent-Muslims. But before being a series of expeditions to regain possession of the Holy Sepulchre that is of Jerusalem, (which had been taken by the Muslims, remember, not by my aunt), the Crusades were the response to four centuries of invasions and occupations. They were a counter-offensive to stem Islamic expansionism in Europe. To deflect it, mors tua vita mea, towards the Orient (meaning India and Indonesia and China) then towards the whole African continent and towards Russia and Siberia where the Tartars converted to Islam were already crushing the followers of Christ. At the conclusion of the Crusades, in fact, the sons of Allah resumed their persecutions as before and more than before.

By the hand of the Turks, this time. The Turks who were about to prepare the birth to the Ottoman Empire. An empire that until 1700 would concentrate on the West all of its greed: turn Europe into its favourite battlefield. Interpreters and bearers of that greed, the famous Janissaries who still today enrich our language with the synonym of killer fanatic assassin. And do you know who the Janissaries actually were? The chosen troops of the Empire, the super-soldiers as capable of self-immolation as of fighting and massacring and sacking. Do you know where they were recruited or rather pressed into service? In the countries subjugated by the Empire. In Greece, for example, or in Bulgaria, in Romania, in Hungary, in Albania, in Serbia. Often in Italy too, along the coasts plied by their pirates. Those coasts where still today you can see the remains of the watchtowers used for spotting their arrival and warning the towns and villages. And where still resounds the echo of the scream which today is used as a mockery but at that time was a cry of terror and despair: «Mamma, li turchi! Mother, the Turks!». They abducted those killers to be at the age of eleven or twelve, together with even younger children to put in the seraglios of the sultans and viziers given to paedophilia, and they chose them from the best-looking and strongest of the important families' firstborns. After the conversion they shut them in the military barracks and here, forbidding them to have any kind of amorous or affectionate relations, marriage included, they indoctrinated them as not even Hitler would indoctrinate his Waffen SS. They turned them into the most formidable fighting machine the world had seen since Roman times.

41

* * *

I don't want to insist too much with this little lesson of history which in our super Politically Correct schools would be a mortal sin but, at least in a summary way, I must refresh the memory of the oblivious and of the hypocrites. So here it is. In 1356, eighty-four years after the Eighth Crusade, the Turks got Gallipoli that is the peninsula stretching for a hundred kilometres along the northern shore of the Dardanelles. From there they marched in conquest of southeast Europe and in the blink of an eye they invaded Thrace, Macedonia, Albania. They subdued Greater Serbia, and with another five-year siege paralyzed Constantinople now cut off from the rest of the West. In 1396 they stopped, it's true, to face the Mongols in their turn Islamized yet rebellious. In 1430 however they resumed their march against us and occupied Venetian Salonika. Crashing aside the Christians at Varna in 1444 they secured possession of Walachia, Moldavia, Transylvania, the territory now called Bulgaria and Romania, then in 1453 they put again under siege Constantinople which on May 29 fell into the hands of Mehmet II and by the way: do you know who was Mehmet II? A guy who, by virtue of the Islamic Fratricide Law which authorized a sultan to murder members of his immediate family, had ascended the throne by strangling his three year-old brother. Do you know the chronicle that about the fall of Constantinople the scribe Phrantzes has left us to refresh the memory of the oblivious or rather of the hypocrites?

Perhaps not. Especially in Europe, a Europe that weeps only for the Muslims, never for the Christians or the Jews or the Buddhists or the Hindus, it would not be Politically Correct to know the details of the fall of Constantinople. Its inhabitants who at daybreak, while Mehmet II is shelling Theodosius' walls, take refuge in the cathedral of St. Sophia and here start to sing psalms. To invoke divine mercy. The patriarch who by candlelight celebrates his last Mass and in order to lessen the panic thunders: «Fear not, my brothers and sisters! Tomorrow you'll be in the Kingdom of Heaven and your names will survive till the end of time!». The children who cry in terror, their mothers who give them heart repeating: «Hush, baby, hush! We die for our faith in Jesus Christ! We die for our Emperor Constantine XI, for our homeland!». The Ottoman troops who beating their drums step over the breaches in the fallen walls, overwhelm the Genovese and Venetian and Spanish defenders, hack them on to death with scimitars, then burst into the cathedral and behead even newborn babies. They amuse themselves by snuffing out the candles with their little severed heads... It lasted from the dawn to the afternoon, that massacre. It abated only when the Grand Vizier mounted the pulpit of St. Sophia and said to the slaughterers: «Rest. Now this temple belongs to Allah». Meanwhile the city burns, the soldiery crucify and hang and impale, the Janissaries rape and butcher the nuns (four thousand in a few hours) or put the survivors in chains to sell them at the market of Ankara. And the servants prepare the Victory Feast. The feast during which (in defiance of the Prophet) Mehmet II got drunk on the wines of Cyprus and, having a soft spot for young boys, sent for the firstborn of the Greek Orthodox Grand Duke Notaras. A fourteen year-old adolescent known for his beauty. In front of everyone he raped him, and after the rape he sent for his family. His parents, his grandparents, his uncles, his aunts and cousins. In front of him he beheaded them. One by one. He also had all the altars destroyed, all the bells melted down, all the churches turned into mosques or bazaars. Oh, yes. That's how Constantinople became Istanbul. But Doudou of the UN and the teachers in our schools don't want to hear about it.

Three years later, that is in 1456, they conquered Athens where once again Mehmet II made mosques of all the churches and... The conquest of Athens completed their invasion of Greece (which they were to hold and ruin for no less than four hundred years). And this conquest was followed by a direct attack to the Venetian Republic which in 1476 saw them advance in Friuli and in the Isonzo Valley. In 1480, they descended again on Puglia and on July 28 the army of Ahmet Pasha landed at Otranto which defended only by the towns folk and by a handful of soldiers fell in the space of two weeks. Here too they burst into the cathedral where they immediately beheaded the Archbishop who was giving the Eucharist. And with the Archbishop, all the priests. They also abducted all the young and beautiful women, threw them to the soldiers, and killed or enslaved the others. Finally they rounded up eight hundred survivors aged fifteen-eighteen and took them to the camp of Ahmet Pasha who presented the following ultimatum: «Do you wish to convert or to die?». «I would rather die» answered the sixteen year-old Antonio Grimaldo Pezzulla, cloth-clipper that is textile worker. Then they all started shouting «me too-me too», and Ahmet Pasha gave them what they wanted by cutting their heads off. At a hundred heads a day. In fact the massacre lasted exactly eight days. Only a certain Mario Bernabei saved himself, by choosing to convert. But he soon proved to be a very poor Muslim and as punishment was impaled. (So Pietro Colonna tells in his *Commenti sull'Apocalisse*).

During the following century, more or less the same. Because in 1512 the Ottoman Empire was taken over by Selim the Grim. Again by virtue of the Fratricide Law he ascended the throne by strangling two brothers plus five nephews plus various caliphs as well as an unspecified number of viziers, and from such a gentleman was born the far-sighted sultan who wanted to create the «Islamic State of Europe»: Süleyman the Magnificent. As soon crowned Sultan, in fact, Süleyman the Magnificent assembled an army of four hundred thousand men and thirty thousand camels plus forty thousand horses and three hundred cannons. From the now-Islamized Romania in 1526 he went into Catholic Hungary and, despite the heroism of the defenders, disintegrated its army in less than forty-eight hours. Then he reached Buda, present-day Budapest. He put it to the torch and guess how many Hungarians (men and women and children) ended up in the slave market that now characterized Istanbul: one hundred thousand.

Guess how many ended up, the following year, in the markets competing with Istanbul. That is, in the bazaars of Damascus and Baghdad and Cairo and Algiers. Three million. But not even this satisfied his cupidity. Because to create the «Islamic State of Europe» he assembled a second army with another four hundred cannons, and in 1529 he moved from Hungary into Austria. The ultra-Catholic Austria that was by now considered the bulwark of Christianity. He didn't succeed in conquering it: that much is true. After five weeks of failed assaults he decided to withdraw. But in his withdrawal he impaled thirty thousand peasants whom he did not consider worthy to be sold as slaves because the price of slaves had dropped as a result of the three million and one hundred thousand ones captured in Hungary. And once back in Istanbul he entrusted the reform of his navy to the famous pirate Khayr Ad-Din known as Barbarossa, Red Beard. The reform enabled to turn the Mediterranean into a watery field of Islam so after foiling a palace plot by ordering the strangulation of his first and second born plus their six children, that is his grandchildren, in 1565 he descended on the Christian stronghold of Malta. And it was totally useless that in 1566 he died (hallelujah!) of a heart attack.

*   *   *

Totally useless because the throne went to his third son known not as «The Magnificent» but as «The Sot». And it was precisely under Selim the Sot that in 1571 General Lala Mustafa conquered the very Christian Cyprus, and here committed one of the most atrocious infamies with which the presumed Ray of Civilization has ever smeared and smudged itself. I mean the martyrdom of Venetian senator Marcantonio Bragadino, Governor of the island. As we are told by historian Paul Fregosi in his extraordinary book *Jihad*, after signing the surrender Bragadino went to Lala Mustafa to discuss peace terms. And, being a stickler for form, he arrived in full pomp. That is, mounting on an exquisitely turned-out steed and wearing the Senate violet robe. In addition, escorted by forty harquebusiers in high uniform and by the strikingly handsome page-boy Antonio Quirini (son of Admiral Quirini) who held a precious parasol over his head. But that time too there was really no talk of peace, my dear pacifists one-way. Because according to a pre-established plan the Janissaries immediately seized the strikingly handsome Antonio. They locked him in the seraglio of Lala Mustafa who deflowered boys with even greater gusto than Mehmet II, then surrounded the forty harquebusiers and hacked them to pieces with their scimitars. Literally to pieces, like the stewed meat. Finally they unhorsed Bragadino, they sliced off his nose and ears forthwith. Then, thus mutilated, they forced him to kneel before the monster who ordered to flay him alive. Along with the execution, the flaying took place thirteen days later, in the presence of the Cypriots who had been compelled to attend. While the Janissaries sneered at his nose-less and ear-less face, Bragadino was made to walk round the town several times dragging bags of rubbish and licking the ground every time that he passed before Lala Mustafa. Then the final torture. He died while being flayed. And when the flaying was over, Lala Mustafa commanded to straw-stuff his skin and fashion a puppet. Always by his order, the puppet was placed astride a cow and one more time circled around the town then hoisted atop the mainmast of his flagship. To the perpetual glory of Islam.

Useless also that on October 7 of the same year a very angry Republic of Venice allied with Spain, with Genova, Florence, Turin, Parma, Mantua, Lucca, Ferrara, Urbino, Malta, the Papacy, and defeated Ali Pasha's navy in the Battle of Lepanto. By this time, in fact, the Ottoman Empire was at the height of its power and under the successive sultans it continued without hinders to attack the continent where Süleyman the Magnificent wanted to settle his «Islamic State of Europe». They reached as far as Poland that the Crescent Moon hordes invaded twice: in 1621 and in 1672... Not by chance, the dream of establishing the «Islamic State of Europe» was halted only in 1683. That is when Grand Vizier Kara Mustafa amassed six hundred thousand soldiers plus a thousand cannons, forty thousand horses, twenty thousand camels, twenty thousand elephants, twenty thousand buffaloes, twenty thousand mules, twenty thousand bulls and cows, ten thousand sheep and goats as well as one hundred thousand sacks of corn and fifty thousand bags of coffee, plus a hundred of wives and concubines. Lugging such a cornucopia he returned to Austria and erecting an immense encampment, (twenty-five thousand tents in addition to his own which was furnished with ostriches and peacocks and fountains), he reached Vienna that for the second time was put under siege.

The fact is that in 1683 Europeans were more intelligent than they are today. And apart from the French who also at that time liked to fornicate with Islam (consider the Treaty of Alliance signed by Louis XIV, le Roi Soleil) but had promised the Austrians to remain neutral, they all rushed to defend the capital by now seen as the bulwark of Christianity. All of them, yes. English, Spanish, Germans, Ukrainians, Poles, Italians. (Meaning Genovese, Venetians, Tuscans, Piedmontese, subjects of the Papal State). On September 12 they scored the extraordinary victory that compelled Kara Mustafa to flee abandoning his camels and his elephants, his buffaloes and his mules, his corn and his coffee, his ostriches and his peacocks, his wives and his concubines... Worse: to prevent his wives and his concubines from falling into the hands of the infidel-dogs, Kara Mustafa had to slit their throats one by one.

What I say is that today's Islamic invasion of Europe is nothing else than a revival of its centuries-old expansionism, of its centuries-old imperialism, of its centuries-old colonialism. More underhand, though. More treacherous. Because this time it is characterized not only by the current Kara Mustafas and Lala Mustafas and Ali Pashas and Ahmet Pashas and Süleymans the Magnificent, that is by the Bin Ladens and the Al Zarkawis and the various Arafats and the butchers who blow themselves up with the skyscrapers or buses. It is characterized also by the immigrants who settle in our countries, our homelands. And who without any respect for our laws impose on us their own laws. Their own customs, their God. Do you know how many of them live in the European continent, that is in the stretch running from the Atlantic coast to the Urals? About sixty million. In the European Union only, about twenty-five. Outside the European Union, thirty-five. Which includes Switzerland where they account for over ten percent of the population, Russia where they account for ten and a half percent, Georgia where they account for twelve percent, the island of Malta where they account for thirteen percent, Bulgaria where they account for fifteen percent. And eighteen percent in Cyprus, nineteen in Serbia, thirty in Macedonia, sixty in Bosnia-Herzegovina, ninety in Albania, ninety-three and a half in Azerbaijan... For the moment they are scarce only in Portugal where they account for 0.50 percent, in Ukraine where they account for 0.45 percent, in Latvia where they account for 0.38 percent, in Slovakia for 0.19 percent, in Lithuania for 0.14 percent, in Iceland for 0.04 percent. (Lucky Icelanders). But everywhere, even in Iceland, they are visibly increasing. And not only because the invasion is proceeding relentlessly but because the Muslims stand as the most prolific ethnic and religious group in the world. A characteristic favoured by polygamy and the fact that in a woman the Koran sees only a womb for giving birth.

* * *

Ah! Touching this subject means risking more than pillory and harassment. It means asking for a life sentence. In our subjugated Europe the Islamic fertility is such a taboo that nobody ever dares to speak about it. If you try, you go straight to court for racism and xenophobia and blasphemy. (Among the charges moved against me at the trial in Paris there was the following sentence of mine: «Ils se multiplient comme les rats. They breed like rats». A little brutal, I agree, but indisputably accurate). The fact is that no trial, no liberticide law, will ever be able to negate what they themselves boast. In the last half-century Muslims have increased by 235 percent. (Christians only by 47 percent). In 1996 there were one billion and 483 million, in 2001 one billion and 624 million. In 2002, one billion and 657 million. And so on. Their world population increases at the rate of thirty-three million a year. Soon it will reach the two billion, and no judge will ever be able to dismiss the figures (supplied by the UN) which attribute to the Muslims a growth fluctuating between 4.60 and 6.40 percent a year. (Christians, only 1.40 percent). To believe it, you only need to remember that the most densely populated regions of the former Soviet Union are the Muslim regions. Starting with Chechnya. That in the Sixties the Muslims of Kosovo were the 60 percent, and in the Nineties the 90 percent. Today, one hundred percent. And no pillory, no harassment, no life-sentence will ever be able to deny that just for this overwhelming fertility in the Seventies and Eighties the Palestinian invaders could take possession of Beirut, thus overpowering the Maronite Christian majority. Still less will it be possible to deny that in the European Union their newborns increase every year for ten percent. In Brussels, as much as thirty percent. In Marseilles, almost seventy percent. And that in various Italian cities the percentage is rising so dramatically that in 2015 the present half a million grandsons of Allah in Italy will be at least two million.

At least two million because, in the elementary schools of the northern regions (for instance in Veneto and Lombardy) fifteen years ago those children were only 30.000. Now they are no less than 100.000. In Piedmont, Liguria, Tuscany, about the same. In Milano they have abundantly overcome the 10 percent of the school population. In Mantua, just the same. In Brescia, last year a school of seven hundred children counted almost four hundred pupils of Albanian or Algerian or Moroccan nationality. And for that ethnic group in Ivrea, Piedmont, a private high school had to

employ Maghrebin teachers. With all the consequent problems. The newcomers, in fact, don't
speak Italian. And teaching them the rudiments of
our language takes four or five months. If they en-
rol after the beginning of the school year, during
lessons they don't understand a word. To say
«open your book» the teacher must mime the ge-
sture of opening a book. Something which goes to
detriment of the Italian children who in order to
follow the program have to wait for their classmates to learn the Italian language. It goes to their detriment also because the real incomprehensions
arise when the teacher faces subjects related to the
humanities. In Europe so deeply connected with
the Christian culture. How to make them understand Dante Alighieri and Alessandro Manzoni?
How to explain them our works of art, the paintings which portray Jesus Christ or the Virgin
Marys and Saints or the naked women like Botti-
celli's Venus? How to speak with them about our
history, for example about the Crusades seen from
our western and therefore Christian standpoint?
Not seldom, some Muslim children protest. They
object that it isn't true, that the Holy Sepulchre
belonged to the Prophet's disciples, that Christ
was a prophet of Islam, that nobody crucified him.
And all this without taking into consideration the
problem of mixed classrooms. I mean the class-

rooms where the Muslim parents don't want to see boys and girls together, the girls don't want to attend the hour of physical education or to undress for swimming. And all this, while the parents of Italian students (or French or British or Spanish etcetera) bleakly complaint: «Do the Muslims have to integrate with us or do we have to integrate with them?!?».

Apparently it is us who have to integrate with them. In 1974 Boumedienne, the man who ousted Ben Bella three years after Algerian Independence, spoke before the General Assembly of the United Nations. And without circumlocutions he said: «One day millions of men will leave the southern hemisphere of this planet to burst into the northern one. But not as friends. Because they will burst in to conquer, and they will conquer by populating it with their children. Victory will come to us from the wombs of our women». Nor did he say something new. Since the night of times the so-called Policy-of-the-Womb, I mean the strategy of exporting human beings and having them breed in abundance, is the simplest way to take possession of a territory. To dominate a country, to replace a population or to subjugate it. And, from the Eighth Century onwards, Islamic expansionism has always unfolded in the shadow of that strategy. Often, through rape and concubinage. Think of what its warriors and occupying troops did in Andalusia, in Albania, in Serbia, in Moldavia, in Bulgaria, in Romania, in Hungary, in Russia, and also in Sicily, in Sardinia, in Puglia, in Provence. Think of what they did in certain parts of Asia. For example in India and even in China. Not to mention Africa, starting with Egypt and the whole Maghreb. However with the decline of the Ottoman Empire the Policy-of-the-Womb had lost its momentum, and Boumedienne's speech was like a clarion-call which should have aroused suspicion even in the oblivious ones. That very same year, in fact, the Islamic Conference concluded its meeting in Lahore with a Resolution which included a plan to turn the then modest flow of immigrants towards Europe and penetrate the continent through «demographic preponderance». A plan that now is a precept. Yes, a precept. In every mosque of Europe the Friday prayer is accompanied by the exhortation with which the imam addresses the Muslim women: «Bear at least five children each couple»... Well: five children each couple is quite a number. In the case of an immigrant with two wives, they become ten. In the case of an immigrant with three wives, they become fifteen. And don't tell me that in Europe polygamy is forbidden by law. Because, if you do, my disdain sprouts and I remind you that if you're an Italian or French or British or German etcetera bigamist, you go straight to prison. But if you are an Algerian or a Moroccan or a Pakistani or a Sudanese or a Senegalese polygamist, no-one touches a hair of your head.

In 1993 France passed a law banning the immigration of polygamists and authorizing the expulsion of those who already lived in the country with more than one wife. But the gurus of Political Correctness and the agitprops of victimism started wailing in the name of Human-Rights and Ethnic-Religious-Plurality. They addressed the lawmakers with the same allegations they now address to me, intolerance, racism, xenophobia, and today in France you find polygamous immigrants all over the place. In the rest of Europe, ditto. Including Italy where Article 556 of the Criminal Code punishes the culprits with up to five years in prison, and where there has never been one single trial or expulsion for polygamy. Not far from my home in Tuscany a Maghrebin lives with two or three wives and a dozen children. (The number of the children is uncertain because every few months another one is born. The number of the wives, because they never go out together and in addition to the chador they wear the nikab. I mean the mask which covers the face to the bridge of the nose. So they all look the same). One day I asked the village police-inspector why his men permitted the Maghrebin to violate Article 556. And the answer was: «For reasons of public order». An euphemism which, translated into simple words, signified: «Not to make out of him an enemy, not to irritate his abettors». In other words, «Because we are afraid».

* * *

Exactly so. Europe burning into torpor like the city of Troy has renewed the disease that last century made Fascists even the Italians who were not Fascists, that made Nazi even the Germans who were not Nazi, that made Bolsheviks even the Russians who were not Bolsheviks, and that now transforms in traitors even those who would not like to be traitors. It is a deadly plague, the fear. A disease which, fed by opportunism and conformism, hence cowardice, leads to more deaths than cancer. It is a disease which unlike cancer is contagious and strikes all those who are along its road. The good and the bad. The intelligent and the stupid. The honest and the dishonest. I have seen terrible things, in the nowadays Eurabia, caused by fear. Things much uglier than those I've seen in war where in fear we live and we die. I've seen leaders who used to pose as Braggarts and who out of fear hoisted (and hoist) the white flag. I've seen liberals who called themselves champions of secularism and who out of fear sang (and sing) the glory of the Koran. I've seen friends or alleged friends who (though cautiously) had sided with me and who out of fear have done an about-turn. They have surrendered and now they are openly against me. But the most terrible thing I've seen has been the fear of those who should protect the freedom of thought and of speech: the journalists, the teachers, the so-called intellectuals.*

Last summer in Florence don Roberto Tassi, parish priest of Santa Maria de' Ricci (the little church where in 1274 Dante Alighieri first saw his beloved Beatrice), put up two moving posters. The first, in front of the main altar. A poster which simply said: «Hail, our Cross, our only hope! Those bearded zealots want to destroy all of us!». The second, in the churchyard along with an image of

* *Note of the Author*. One of them is an old and pompous Italian who pontificating about democracy used to teach Political Science at the Columbia University of New York: real nest of illiberal liberals. A former admirer of my work and now a champion of opportunism, conformism, fear, he has become a most hysterical and bilious aggressor of mine. He recently wrote, for instance, that the syllogism I mention in the next page is not a syllogism.

the disintegrated Twin Towers. A poster which offered a perfect syllogism: «Islam is theocracy. Theocracy denies democracy. Ergo, Islam is against democracy». Don Tassi is a likeable and peculiar priest. A guy who wears the cassock exclusively to say Mass, who dresses like a peasant in the field, and who in his Sunday sermons says things of this kind: «Dear folks, atheism has done the Church a real favour. Because it has removed the Church's temporal power and compelled us to deal with God and nothing else». Or: «Forget angels and archangels flapping around heaven. Angels do not exist. Only Jesus Christ exists. Jesus, the son of Our Father and the teacher of freedom». Or: «Let's say it loud and clear. Democracy has opened men's eyes no less than the Gospels». In short, what is in his heart is on his tongue. And among the truths which are in his heart therefore on his tongue there is the truth about Islam. A topic on which he is a real scholar. His humble house overflows with books on the matter and his opinion on it never fails: «Islam a meek and merciful religion? Come on, folks. Either one is a Muslim or not. If he is, he must obey the Koran. And for sure the Koran is not a meek and merciful book». Well: don Tassi put those two moving posters inside and outside the Santa Maria church to explain in his simple way that theocracy keeps in ignorance, deprives of conscience, kills the intellect. And any secular person should have thanked him for this. For Christsake, it isn't easy to find a priest to whom secular principles are dearer than catechism. But led by one of the bellicose pacifists who in 2002 wanted to smear the monuments of Florence, (this time a French), the rainbow-flaggers forced him to take down the posters. Without a single person raising its voice to defend him, of course. As for the media, well: in Rome a daily paper reported the news with this headline: «Crusade against Islam». In Florence, with this headline: «Stop the anti-Islam priest». In fact in the dream that the sons of Allah have been cultivating for so long, the dream of blowing up Giotto's Tower and the Tower of Pisa and the dome of St. Peter or the Eiffel Tower and the Big Ben and so forth, I see more foolishness than strategy... What sense would there be in destroying the treasures of a society that in the substance already belongs to them? A society where the Koran is the new Das Kapital. Mohammed, the new Karl Marx. Bin Laden, the new Lenin. And September 11 the new Taking of the Bastille, of the Winter Palace.

CHAPTER 2

That their dream of destroying the Eiffel Tower came from a gross foolishness not a strategy, became clear to me in the late spring of 2002. Namely when the *The Rage and the Pride* was published in France where a novelist had just been charged for saying that the Koran is the most stupid and dangerous book in the world, and where in 1997 then in 1998 then in 2000 then in 2001 Brigitte Bardot had been convicted for writing what she never tires of repeating. That the Muslims have stolen her homeland. That even in the remotest villages French churches have been replaced by mosques and the Lord's Prayer by the muezzins' caterwauling. That even in democratic regimes there is a limit to tolerance, that halal butchery is barbaric. (By the way: it is. To the same extent as shechitah or kosher butchery. I mean the Jewish practice of slitting the animals' throats without stunning them and then letting them die little by little, drained of their blood, drop by drop. So when all the blood has flown down, the meat is «pure». Nice and white, pure...).

I understood it, in short, before being indicted in France as the novelist and Brigitte Bardot. Because do you know who was the Holy Office that piled up the firewood for my stake? The Paris weekly to which my French publisher had mindlessly granted the advance excerpts: *Le Point*. And you know how *Le Point* piled up the firewood? By publishing, alongside my text, the prosecutorial comments of the various French Fra' Accursios: journalists, psychoanalysts, philosophers or pseudo-philosophers, politologists or everythingologists. (Not seldom, with Arab names. Rather often, with Jewish names). And do you know who lit the fire? The Extreme Left magazine which put on the front cover the headline of the article-censure: «Anatomie d'un Livre Abject. Anatomy of an Abject Book». Do you know what happened right after? It happened that although the abject-book was selling like hot-cakes in every bookshop, many sons of Allah demanded to remove it from the shop-windows and from the shelves, thus many frightened booksellers were forced to sell it under the counter. As for the trial, it was triggered not only by the complaint filed by the Muslims of the «Mrap» (Mouvement contre le Racisme et pour l'Amitié entre les Peuples), but also by the complaint filed by the Jews of the «Licra» (Ligue Internationale contre le Racisme et l'Antisémitisme). The Muslims of the «Mrap», demanding that every copy be confiscated and (I suppose) burned. The Jews of the «Licra», demanding that every copy bear a warning similar to the one which defaces cigarette-packs: «Attention! This book may damage your mental health». Both of them, demanding that I be sentenced to a year in prison plus to a heavy amercement to fill their pockets... Thanks to a wrong procedural technicality, I was not condamned: it's known. And the two appeals which followed the sentence were rejected on the basis that the book had become at once a bestseller, thus any renewal of the trial would be a loss of time. But this did not delete the fact that the leftist Jews of «Licra» had alined against me with the Muslims of «Mrap». A senseless wickedness which at that time I did not understand. Now, on the contrary, I do.

I do because, even if your grandparents died at Dachau or Mauthausen, it is not easy to be brave in a country where there are around ten million Muslims and more than three thousand mosques. Where Islamic racism and hatred for infidel-dogs prevails but is never brought to trial, never condamned. Where many Muslims declare: «We must take advantage of the democratic space France offers us. We must exploit democracy and use it to occupy territory». Where as many of them add: «In Europe Nazi ideas were not understood. Or not by everyone. They were considered a homicidal madness, yet Hitler was a great man». Where all of them would like to abolish the article of the French Constitution which since 1905 separates the Church from the State. And with that article the laws which forbid polygamy, wife repudiation, religious proselytism in schools. Where ten years ago a French-Turkish girl of Colmar was stoned by her mother and father and brothers and uncles because she had fallen in love with a Catholic and wanted to marry him. («Better dead than dishonoured» was that family's comment). Where in November 2001, just two months after September 11, a French-Moroccan girl of Galeria, Corsica, was stabbed to death with twenty-four knife-wounds by her father because she was about to marry a Corsican who was also Catholic. («Better a life sentence than dishonour» was the father's comment at the arrest). Where as early as 1994 a stylist of Maison Chanel had to offer an official apology to the Muslim communities as well as destroy dozens of marvellous dresses because his summer collection featured cloths embroidered or printed with decorative verses from the Koran and in Arabic. Where recently a Catholic farmer was ordered to remove the cross he kept in a cornfield (a field belonging to him) because «the sight of that religious symbol caused tension with the Muslims». Where Islamic arrogance would like to ban from

66

schools the «blasphemous» works of Voltaire and Victor Hugo. With those blasphemous texts, the teaching of biology: a science they consider «immodest because it deals with the human body and sex». With the teaching of biology, gymnastics and swimming lessons. Both sports which cannot be practised wearing a burka or a chador.

It's even less easy to be a hero in a country where, in some cities, Muslims are not the official ten-percent of the population but the twenty or thirty or more. If you don't believe it, go to Lyon or Lille or Roubaix or Bordeaux or Rouen or Limoges or Nice or Toulouse or better still to Marseilles which is no longer a French city. It's an Arab city, a Maghrebin city. Go and look at the highly central quarter of Bellevue Pyat, now a slum of filth and delinquency, a kasbah where on Fridays you cannot even walk in the streets because the great mosque does not have enough room and many pray in the open air. (But the police refuse to venture saying: «C'est trop dangereux. It's too dangerous»). Go and look at the famous Rue du Bon Pasteur where each woman is veiled, each man wears djellabah and long beard and turban, and from morning till night idles in front of a TV set showing programmes in Arabic. Go and look at the Collège Edgard Quinet where ninety-five percent of the pupils are Muslims and where last year a fifteen year-old girl by the name of Nyma was savagely beated by her classmates and thrown into a garbage-bin because she was wearing blue jeans. In the bin she also risked being burned. I say «risked» because she was saved by the college principal, Jean Pellegrini, who got two stab-wounds for his pains. (Know who stabbed him? Nyma's brother). Yes, now I do understand those ungrateful Jews of «Licra». Now I do. Collabora-tionism is almost always born of fear. Yet their ca-se reminds me of the German Jewish bankers who, hoping to save themselves, in the Thirties lent money to Hitler. And who, despite this, en-ded up in the ovens.

This said, let's deal with Westminster Abbey.

* * *

That the dream of destroying Westminster Abbey was another gross foolishness became clear to me on the spring of 2003, when the *London Times* published an essay in which I thunde-red against European anti-Americanism and at the same time I expressed my doubts about the op-portunity of waging war on Saddam Hussein. We fight this war to free Iraq, Bush and Blair had said. We fight to bring democracy and freedom to Iraq as at the time of Hitler and Mussolini we fought to bring democracy and freedom to Europe and to Japan. And in my essay I objected: you're wrong. Freedom and democracy are not two pieces of chocolate to give as a gift to those who don't know them and don't want to know them. In Europe the operation succeeded because in Europe the two pieces of chocolate were a food we knew well, a heritage we had built and lost, thus we wanted them back and with you we fought to have them back. In Japan it succeeded because Japan had already begun the march towards progress in the second half of the 19th century. As a consequence, Japanese were ready to eat the two never tested pieces of chocolate. To understand what they meant, and to eat them. Freedom and democracy have to be wanted. And in order to want them you have to know what they are. You have to understand their concepts. Ninety-five percent of Muslims reject freedom and democracy not only because they don't know what they are but because they don't understand their concepts. Because their concepts are too strongly opposed to those on which theocratic totalitarianism is based. Too opposite, antithetical, to Islamic ideology. In that ideology it's God who commands. Not men. It's God who decides human destiny. Not men. A God who leaves no room for choice, for common sense, for reasoning. A God to whom men are not even sons: they are subjects, slaves. Mr. Bush, Mr. Blair, do you really believe that in Baghdad the Iraqis will welcome your troops with hugs and kisses, flowers and applauses, meaning how sixty years ago we welcomed them in Europe? And even if this happened, (in Baghdad anything can happen), what will happen next? In their last «elections», over two-thirds of Iraqis gave Saddam Hussein «the hundred percent» of votes, and now their real intention is to set up an Islamic Republic of Iraq. A regime modelled on the Islamic Republic of Iran. And what if instead of discovering the concepts of freedom and democracy Iraq becomes a second Vietnam? What if instead of installing a Pax Americana that hypothetical second Vietnam spreads and the entire Middle East blows up? Yes, I have many doubts on this war. In my opinion, it would be wiser to let the Iraqis stew in their own juice.

I also voiced the dread that president Bush would take such a risk to keep a filial promise made after the Gulf War, meaning when Saddam Hussein tried to assassinate his father. («Dad, if I too get president, I'll avenge you. I'll make the bastard kneel, I swear on the Bible»). And even though it was a long essay, the *London Times* gave it a high profile. But this took place under the shield of the Political Correctness called objectivity. Meaning, behind the hypocrisy used to neutralize every attitude taken, the tartuffery used to smuggle submission. To turn information into disinformation. Along with my text, in fact, they published photos taken during an ultra-leftist peace demonstration in Rome. And one of these photos showed three imbeciles holding up a poster with the drawing of an Amanita Phalloides: the mushroom whose high concentration of amatoxins sends you straight back to the Creator. Under the cap of the baleful fungus, meaning at the top of the stalk, a picture of my severed head. Above my severed head, the words: «Amanita Fallaci». At the bottom, meaning at the root of the stalk, a skull with crossbones. Beside the skull, the words «Deadly-Poisonous». And under that photo, at the foot of the page, a demented attack written by the Secretary of the Muslim Council of Britain (imam Iqbal Sacranie) with the title: «Miss Fallaci, your views are an insult to peaceful Muslims».

But does this really come as any surprise? With Islam the *London Times* has always been generous. Prodigal, magnanimous. As early as the Eighties, it hosted warnings such as the one addressed by the Superintendent of the London Central Mosque to Margaret Thatcher to inform her that «Muslims in the United Kingdom would not tolerate much longer the foreign policy with which the Prime Minister offended their pan-Islamic feelings».* But listen: to understand what is happening on the other side of the English Channel all you have to do is stop for a few minutes at Speaker's Corner in Hyde Park, where anybody can harangue from a podium and say whatever he wants. In the good old days you would see socialists who spoke about socialism, feminists who spoke about feminism, atheists who spoke about atheism. Now, instead, you see aspiring suicide bombers or mullahs who in the name of freedom of thought (denied to me even by the posters with the Ammanita Fallaci) exalt the Jihad and call for the murder of the infidel-dogs. (Of the infidel-bitches too). You have also to observe the female «bobbies», I mean the London's policewomen. Today many of them are Muslims, (municipal policy requires their recruitment in large numbers), and only rarely do they wear the traditional regulation headgear. They almost always replace it with a hijab, the cloth covering the hair and the forehead and the ears and

* *Note of the Author*. I remind the reader that after the London attack of July 7th 2005, the *London Times* published a cartoon where an Islamic terrorist and an Anglo-American military appeared identically dressed and holding an identical bomb. Over them, the title «See the difference».

the neck... Finally, you have to remember that the strategic base of the Islamic offensive in Europe is not France with its Marseilles and its official ten percent of Muslims: it's Britain with its two and a half percent. Because it is Britain, not France, that shelters the brains, the leaders, of the Islamic offensive. The theologists and ideologists who theorize it. The imams who run it. The politicians who support it. The journalists and the intellectuals and the publishers who propagandize it. The oil-bankers and the moneybags who finance it. I mean the sheikhs, the emirs, the sultans who own the finest buildings and hotels in London.

London (but the other major cities of England are no less) is also home to the most dangerous terrorists in the world. Members of Al Qaeda or Al Ansar or Hamas who even the most Islamized France has expelled. Murderers whose countries of origin, (such as Egypt or Algeria or Tunisia or Morocco), for years have been asking the British Minister of Justice to extradite and whom the Minister of Justice refuses to hand over because they are «political refugees» or naturalized citizens. (One is the imam of the Finsbury Mosque who seventeen years ago participated in the assassination of four European hostages kidnapped by Yemenite terrorists of Sana). All of this without considering the too many Pakistani and Afghan

73

and Jordanian and Palestinian and Sudanese and Senegalese and Maghrebin immigrants who live in Britain on residence permits. Two million, as things stand today. Over 700.000 in the capital only, and all of them people who have not the slightest intention to integrate. Because there the Political Correctness preaches a multiethnic, multireligious, multicultural society. But there too the Muslims respond by fighting in defence of their own identity. The identity that we do not defend. There too they want no part in the process of integration. Just think of the «Muslim Parliament of Great Britain», the gang which always reminds the Islamic immigrants that they are not required to abide by British laws. «*For a Muslim, the observance of his host country's laws is optional. A Muslim must obey the Sharia and the Sharia alone*» says its Founding Charter. In fact on December 20th 1999 the Sharia Court issued a fatwa forbidding all Muslims to take any part in the celebration of Christmas, then reminded that «the Muslim Parliament of Great Britain» wants the «Islamic State of Great Britain». Meaning a State which allows the legalization of polygamy, the replacement of divorce with repudiation, the abolition of gender integration not only in schools but at workplaces and on public transport. Trains, planes, ships, boats, coaches, buses, trams, elevators. Yes, elevators too. (In other words, a segregation substantially identical to the segregation which was in act when American blacks were segregated from American whites). And naturally the Muslim Parliament of Great Britain also wants to convert as many Christians as possible. Through mixed marriages, to begin with. The marriages that imams encourage because a mixed marriage imposes on the non-Muslim spouse the conversion to Islam. It also wants the progeny to be educated under the Sharia as well as exercising, when adults, the work of proselytism and indoctrination. (Besides, this second activity is exercised by all converts. Think of the former rock star Cat Stevens, now Yusuf Islam. After repudiating rock, Mister Cat Stevens-Yusuf Islam has composed nothing but music dedicated to the Prophet. He has also been running four Koran schools that British government subsidizes as a tribute to multiculturalism).

* * *

As for Germany which with its two thousand mosques and its three million Muslim Turks looks like a branch office of the defunct Ottoman Empire, well... The Pan American airliner that in 1988 exploded in mid-air and fell on the Scottish town of Lockerbie killing 270 people had left from Frankfurt: right or wrong? The bomb in the luggage-van had been put in Frankfurt by sons of Allah living in Frankfurt: right or wrong? Mohammed Atta, the commander of the nineteen kamikazes who materialized the September 11 bloodbath, lived in Germany where he had graduated in architecture at the Hamburg Polytechnic: right or wrong? Before going to America to attend flying school in Florida, he had studied as a pilot at the Bonn Flying Club: right or wrong? The money to pay his flying courses in Florida had been withdrawn from a bank in Düsseldorf: right or wrong? And the bulk of Egyptian and Maghrebin and Palestinian terrorists and the Al Qaeda's logistic headquarters have been always located in Germany: right or wrong?

That the dream of destroying Cologne cathedral was as senseless as destroying Westminster Abbey and the Eiffel Tower became clear to me, however, only when I learnt that the most important political refugee in that city was Rabah Kabir: the guy still accused of carrying out the 1992 massacre at the Algiers airport. Despite extradition requests repeatedly submitted by the Algerian government, in fact, in Germany Rabah Kabir is granted political asylum. And in Cologne, where he lives, he has won even a chair in theology. Better, he has even become a high-ranking official in the Islamo-European Union... That the Dresden Masters Picture Gallery was at minor risk than the Cologne cathedral, instead, is something that occurred to me when I read that in eight elementary schools of Lower Saxony the Koran teaching had been introduced and I saw the photo accompanying the news. It was a photograph of two Turkish girls, supposedly born and brought up in Dresden or in Meissen or around there. The elder of the two, eight or nine years old, wearing a T-shirt with a showy «Air Force» printed on the front and an enormous watch at her wrist. The younger, six or seven years old, a very western cardigan. Both of them, however, were muffled up to the shoulders in a merciless hijab. I mean: even though their parents came from the country which Atatürk had secularized eighty years before, both wore the veil that the Koran imposes from the age of seven. And don't forget that in Turkey, (that Turkey so anxious to enter the European Union), the hijab is now displayed again by almost all the women of the new generation. Don't forget that in Turkey, (that Turkey which the German and French and Italian leaders are so anxious to bring into the European Union), episodes worthy of the Marcantonio Bragadino's flayer still take place. Last year in Yaylim, a Turkish village on the Syrian border, thirty-five year-old Cemse Allak was stoned to death by her family because after being raped she had become pregnant. The pregnancy was in its eighth month when they stoned her. And her sister-in-law's comment was: «What were we supposed to do? She was a spinster and as such she had lost her honour». Her brother's comment was: «Rape or no rape, she dishonoured us». Yet in Germany the Islamic mafia constrains the immigrants workers to deduct from their wages the so-called Revolutionary Tax. A tax which is used to finance the mother-country's political parties. That is, the reactionary parties bent on sweeping away the Atatürk revolution.

The same applies to Holland. That Holland where each year thirty or forty thousand Muslims irrupt, and in Dutch they don't even learn the word «bedankt». (Thank you). That Holland where since 1981 Muslims have had their own quarters, their own trade unions, their own schools, their own hospitals, their own cemeteries, and where mosques are built at government expenses. Where, not satisfied with those privileges, Muslims fill the squares of The Hague to insult the government because the government does not let them bring all their polygamic wives in. And where, if a Mr. Fortuyn runs for election, he ends up assassinated... Where, if a movie director named Theo van Gogh makes a documentary on the status of Muslim women, get slaughtered as a pig by a Muslim.* The same also applies to Denmark where the «political asylum» is granted to the most wanted thugs of Algeria or Tunisia or Pakistan or Sudan with the same insouciance as in Britain and Germany. And where for the last decade the Danes have been converting in droves... The same also applies to Sweden where neither my publisher nor any other publisher has had the courage to publish *The Rage and the Pride* or the other books but, on the contrary, texts singing the praises of Islam fill the bookshops like sardines in a can of sardines. Where Swedish citizenship is granted to anybody who whispers Allah-akbar. Where Stockholm's most illustrious naturalized Swede is Moroccan Ahmed Rami, an ideologue of the Worldwide Islamic Revolution. Thus, ruthless anti-American and ferocious anti-Israeli and hand-in-glove with Swedish neo-Nazis.

* *Note of the Author*. The well known assassination of Theo van Gogh is told and discussed in the third book of this Trilogy on Islam and the West. That is, in the book entitled *Oriana Fallaci interviews herself – The Apocalypse* and not yet translated in English.

But above all, this applies to Spain. That Spain where from Barcelona to Madrid, from San Sebastian to Valladolid, from Alicante to Jerez de la Frontera, you find the best-trained terrorists in the continent. (No coincidence that in July 2001, namely before settling in Miami, the neoarchitect-graduate Mohammed Atta stepped in Spain to visit his explosive-expert buddy detained in Tarragona). And where from Malaga to Gibraltar, from Cadiz to Seville, from Cordoba to Granada, the Moroccan nabobs and the Saudi royals and the Gulf-State emirs have bought the finest lands in the region. Here they finance propaganda and proselytism, reward with six thousand dollars all converts who give birth to a male child. With a thousand dollars, girls and little girls who wear the hijab. That Spain where almost all Spaniards still believe in the myth of Andalusia's Golden Age, of Cordoba's splendours, and see in the Moorish past a Paradise Lost. That Spain where a political movement called «Association for the Return of Andalusia to Islam» exists. And where in the historical quarter of Albaicin, just a few yards from the convent of cloistered nuns serving St. Thomas, last year the Grand Mosque of Granada and its annexed Islamic Center were inaugurated. An event made possible by the Memorandum of Understanding signed in 1992 by the socialist Felipe González to guarantee full legal recognition to Muslims in Spain. A masochism realized with the billions paid by Libya, Malaysia, Saudi Arabia, Brunei, and by the scandalously rich Sultan of Sharjah whose son opened the ceremony declaring: «I am here with the emotion of a man who returns to his homeland». So the Spanish converts (two thousand in Granada alone) echoed with the shout: «We are rediscovering our roots!».

* * *

Perhaps because eight centuries of Muslim subjugation are hard to digest and too many Spaniards still have the Koran in their blood, Spain is the European country where Islamization occurs with more spontaneity. It's also the country where that process has been going on longest. As explained by the French geopolitical analyst Alexandre Del Valle who on the Islamic offensive and Islamic totalitarianism has written important books, (of course execrated and denigrated and crucified by the Politically Correct), the «Association for the Return of Andalusia to Islam» was founded in Cordoba no less than thirty years ago. And it was not founded by the sons of Allah. It was founded by the Spaniards of the Extreme Left who, disillusioned with the embracing of bourgeois values by the proletariat, had discovered the God of the Koran moved from Prophet Marx to Prophet Mohammed. The Moroccan nabobs and the Saudi royals and the Gulf-State emirs immediately rushed to bless them with money, and the association bloomed. It did so enriched with apostates who came from Barcelona, from Guadalajara, from Valladolid, from Ciudad Real, from León, but also from Britain. Also from Sweden. Also from Denmark. Also from Italy. Also from Germany. Also from America. Without any intervention on the part of the governments, no. And without any alarm on the part of the Catholic Church. In 1979, in the name of ecumenism, the Bishop of Cordoba even went as far as allowing them to celebrate the Feast of the Sacrifice (the one in which lambs are slaughtered in droves) inside his cathedral. «We-are-all-brothers». The concession caused some problems: crucifixes dislodged, Madonnas knocked over, lambs' offal thrown into the fonts. Thus the following year the repentant prelate sent them to Seville. But here they dropped right into the middle of Holy Week, and listen to me. If there is anything in the world more dismaying than the Islamic Feast of the Sacrifice, this is the Seville Holy Week's Procession. Its passing bells. Its lugubrious processions. Its macabre Via

Crucis. Its self-flagellating Nazarenos. Its hooded ranks that advance rolling the death-announcing drums. As a consequence...

Shouting «Long-live-Islamic-Andalusia, down-with-Torquemada, Allah-will-triumph» the newly converted Brothers in Mohammed threw themselves on their former Brothers in Christ, and fists started flying. Result, the Brothers in Prophet Mohammed had to clear out of Seville too. They moved to Granada where they settled in the historical quarter of Albaicin, and this is the point. Because despite the naïve anti-clericalism spit up during the Holy Week Procession, those Brothers in Prophet Mohammed were not naïve at all. In Granada they created a situation similar to the one which at the time was engulfing Beirut and which now is engulfing so many cities of France, Britain, Germany, Italy, Holland, Sweden, Denmark, etcetera. Ergo, today the quarter of Albaicin is in every sense a State within the State. An Islamic feud, an apostatic domain, which lives with its own laws. Its own institutions, its own hospital, its own cemeteries. Its own abattoir, its own newspaper: *La Hora del Islam*. Its own publishers, its own libraries, its own schools. Schools that exclusively teach how to memorize the Koran. And its own shops, of course. Its own markets, its own banks. Even its own currency, given that in Albaicin all is bought and sold with the gold and silver coins struck on the model of the *dirham* in use at the time of Boabdil Lord of old Granada. (Money coined in Calle San Gregorio that for the usual reasons of «public order» the Spanish Ministry of Finance pretends to know nothing about). And from all this comes the question that has been tormenting me over these last years: but how did we get to such a senseless mess? Can tolerance or naïveté or stupidity or misused freedom, misused democracy, bring a civilized society that far?

Before giving an answer, however, I must get back to Italy where thanks to a television programme that left me dumbstruck, in the autumn of 2002 I had the bitter confirmation of how deep was the abyss in which we were plunging.

CHAPTER 3

He was a corpulent Senegalese, about forty years old and self-proclaimed imam of Carmagnola: the little Piedmontese town that in 1400 became famous as the birthplace of captain Francesco Bussone nicknamed Il Carmagnola and that today holds the sad record of having at least one Muslim every ten inhabitants. His name was Abdul Qadir Fadl Allah Mamour, and a few years earlier he had enjoyed a moment of celebrity as the polygamous husband of two Italian citizens. An offence extinguished by the divorce from his first wife but for which, during the triple cohabitation, nobody had dared to arrest him. Now the celebrity was dued to his presumed friendship with Bin Laden, (newspapers used to call him Bin-Laden's-Ambassador-in-Italy), and to his crafty management of immigrants' money. In fact he was the owner of the prosperous finance group called Private Banking Fadl Allah Islamic Investment Company. But, that evening, I knew nothing of this. So when he appeared on the TV screen I wondered who he was, and watched him only because he bore a striking resemblance to Wakil Motawakil: the Taliban minister of Justice who in Kabul used to order the executions of Afghan women guilty of going to the hairdresser's. The same big fat bearded face. The same cruel little eyes, the same belly as swollen as the belly of a pregnant woman. The same black turban, the same djellabah down to his feet. The only difference stood in his voice, slightly less strident.

The programme had already begun, and it seemed broadcast from a poor peasant's slum, certainly not from the house of the Private Banking Fadl Allah Islamic Investment Company's owner. A tele-journalist was interviewing him off camera, and in bad Italian Wakil Motawakil's double answered: «I am investing money from Switzerland to Malaysia, from Singapore to South Africa. Muslim money which is coming out of oil. The great gift that Allah has left to us Muslims and which is called oil. Does Osama supply me with money? If he does, it depends on him that I say it or not. If he wants, I say it. If he does not, I don't say it. But one thing I say: he gives and has given money to many many persons of the West». He also said he knew Osama rather well, that he had met him for the first time in 1994 in the Ivory Coast and then seen him again in the Sudan. He described him as a «man of great intelligence, great religiousness, great humility, a benefactor of whom nobody could speak badly». And in an ecstatic, almost homosexual tone, extolled his good looks. His very sweet and severe eyes. His thin and soft but cold hands. His quick and light walk. «Like a cat». He also said that in Italy the handsome Osama had two thousand Jihad fighters trained in Afghanistan or elsewhere and kept in-order-to-maintain-a-logistic-base-in-the-country, prepare-the-universal-revolution. «To avoid suspicion they act as normal people, working and living with their families just like anybody else. And some of them are well specialized in sabotage» he explained. And then: «See, only four or five or even three mujahidin are enough to destroy cities like London. To paralyze it for thirty-four hours». He also threatened us Italians. He said that our authorities should stop persecuting and oppressing the immigrants like Sharon oppresses the Palestinians or Putèn (read Putin) oppresses the Chechens and Buss (read Bush) oppresses the Muslims of America. Otherwise, he concluded, what had happened with the Twin Towers in America would happen in Italy too. «Wherever-there-is-injustice-and-oppression, there-will-be-sooner-or-later-vendetta».

Yet it wasn't those words that made my blood run cold. It wasn't the arrogance with which he spoke or the impudence with which he chose the words. It was what happened afterwards. Because, afterwards, the scene shifted from the slum house to a decorous office where, seated at a table, you saw the imam of Turin. Meaning the Moroccan Bouriqi Bouchta, the pious lambs-slaughterer who in Turin owns four halal butcher-shops and as many mosques.* Beside him, a very worried gentleman who soon turned out to be the leftist mayor of Carmagnola. On the table, the model of an urban development project. While the pious lambs-slaughterer nodded complacently Abdul Qadir Fadl Allah Mamour revealed what the urban development project was, and guess what it was: the miniature, the facsimile of «the first Islamic City in Italy». A city inhabited exclusively by Muslims, completely self-financed and rationally developed. Squares, streets, bridges, parks. Mosques, Koran schools, Koran libraries. Private banks, hospitals, Sharia police stations, halal supermarkets. And to start

---

* *Note of the Author.* In September 2005, exactly two months after the July 7 attack of London, the pious lambs-slaughterer has been finally expelled from Italy as «a serious perturber of the public order and a danger for the security of the State». His wife (pregnant) followed him with the progeny.

with, three big buildings with forty-eight apartments each. Buildings for which there was an immediate urgency because, Abdul Qadir Etcetera
explained, in Italy the Muslims reached already
the number of one million two hundred thousand. At least thirty thousand were in the nearby
Turin, and every day there were several hundreds
of arrivals from abroad.

Another Albaicin, in short. Another State
within the State. A separate republic that is a kind
of San Marino with minarets instead of belltow-
wers, harems instead of nightclubs, the Sharia instead of our Constitution, and Senegalese or Sudanese or Maghrebins etcetera instead of the Car-
magnolese evicted from their homes. Evicted and
confined to some reservation like the Cherokee
of Oklahoma, the Apache of Dakota, the Navajo
of Arizona, etcetera. Not at random the mayor
looked very worried and all of a sudden, deaf to
the protests of the pious lambs-slaughterer, he
mumbled that such project needed a more care-
ful thought. Before the meeting he had no idea
that Mr. Mamour's project was so colossal, and
for sure the birth of the First Islamic City in Italy
would alter the life of Carmagnola... Then the
scene changed again. The camera framed again
the slum house, and on the screen appeared a large bundle. A package of dark gray cloth from the

top of which a sort of black mask hung. A chador, in short, completed by the nikab. That is, the short veil which hides the face from the bridge of the nose downwards. Between the upper edge of the nikab and the strip of chador lowered over the forehead, two eyes. Inside the dark gray bundle, a body with a pair of black gloves poked out. An Afghan woman, perhaps? A future tenant to whom Wakil Motawakil's double had promised one of the one hundred and forty highly urgently needed apartments?

I thought this until the off-camera journalist informed us that the package of cloth contained or rather was the now only wife of Abdul Qadir Etcetera, as well as the mother of his five children, and through the nikab filtered a voice that in an arrogant tone declaimed: «My name is Aisha and I converted to Islam eight and a half years ago, after studying Arabic at the Milano University. I am from Milano. My family of origin lives in Milano where my Italian parents grew me up as Barbara Farina». So I started to listen very carefully, even more carefully than I had listened to her husband's grim urban development project, and what she said from that moment on shocked me so that until dawn I kept repeating to myself: it is not possible, it is not possible, I must be the victim of a hallucination. Because what this Italian born in Italy (not in Afghanistan) and grown up in Milano (not in Kabul) had said did not fit at all the general belief that Islamic terrorism is a lunatic fringe of benevolent Islam. A blameworthy distortion of a merciful religion and of a shining civilization. On the contrary it confirmed the truths I sustain when the traitors accuse me of racism and xenophobia and blasphemy, when they put me under trial for vilification of Islam and instigation to hate... Bin Laden, she had said, is not a lonely outcast with a handful of followers: he is the heir of Prophet Mohammed, the new leader of the Muslims. He acts on behalf of and at the behest of the Umma, that is, of Islamic world. Here is why the Muslims love him so much and see in him a holy man, a saint, a brother, a hero. Here is why, in reality, we do not need to pulverize your skyscrapers or destroy your monuments. All we need is to exploit your weakness and our prolification.

She had said it in a coarse, oversimplified manner. Don't get me wrong: dialectics was not her natural skill. Polished language, even less. But she had said it in clearness, without a shadow of ambiguity, and with the assurance of a person who states a belief born by an irrefutable fact. Then, in sloppy Italian, she had concluded: «One day Rome will be a domain, the domain, of Islam.

In a sense, by the way, it already is. There are so many Muslims, there. So many. Besides, we are everywhere. Thousands and thousands, millions. But you shouldn't be frightened. This doesn't mean we want to conquer you with armies, with weapons. We don't need it, I repeat. In the end, we don't need your conversions either. Because whereas you are halved, you are in zero growth. On the contrary, we are as fertile as a soil well manured. At each generation we grow. Day by day we double, and more than double».

This upset me a lot, yes. And such emotion increased when I found out that she had been the first Italian woman to wear a nikab in public, the first to keep nikab on in photos for identity papers, the first to admit to a polygamous marriage. It upset me even more when I discovered that to impose Islam on us she did not rely only upon Muslim fertility: her main labor was a monthly publication called «Al Mujahida, The Female Fighter» where she constantly implored Allah to produce millions and millions of «martyrs». That is, kamikazes. In fact I felt most relieved when the Italian government finally decided that Abdul Qadir Etcetera was not only an unpleasant guest but also an Al Quaeda official. As such he was expelled, sent back to Senegal, where Barbara-Aisha followed him with her bellicosity and the five children. And yet what troubles me mostly are not the cases like the one of that disagreable couple. It is the subtle and crawling way with which the Islamic community tries to penetrate the European society, to take possession of it. This, beginning with the demand, the claim, to vote in our elections.

* * *

They demand it as something which is dued to them by Allah. And not only for those who have the Residence Card but, very often, also for those who came illegally and should be expelled. They claim it with such impudent overbearingness that all over Europe the «natives» ask what is the point of being citizens, of having the rights of citizens, where the rights of citizens end and where the rights of foreigners begin. Whether foreigners have the right to exact rights which deny the rights of citizens. In short, whether foreigners count for more than citizens. Whether foreigners are a kind of super-citizens. A question that in Italy, for instance, has reached dramatic proportions.

Enough with nonsense and cheating: the Italian Constitution unequivocably stipulates that the right to vote belongs to citizens and nobody else. «All citizens, men and women, who have rea-

93

ched the age of eighteen are voters. The vote is personal, equal, free and secret. Its exercise is a civic duty» says its Article 48. And not a word about the vote for foreigners. The following articles, ditto. Nor is it clear why they should. It's not the up to foreigners to choose the representatives of the country that gives them hospitality. I don't vote in America. Not even to elect the mayor of New York, even though I reside in New York and pay a ton of taxes. And I judge it fair, correct. Why on earth should I vote in a country of which I am not a citizen?!? I do not vote in France or in Britain or in Belgium or in Holland or in Denmark, in Sweden, in Germany, in Spain, in Portugal, in Greece etcetera, even though my passport bears the words «European Union». And for the same reasons I judge it fair, correct. But in one of its articles the Treaty of Maastricht «contemplates» the alleged right of immigrants to vote and be elected in local councils and European elections. And the Resolution passed on January 15th 2003 by the European Parliament «welcomes» the idea, recommends that member States extend the right to vote to non-EU citizens who have been resident for at least five years. A right (or rather an alleged right) that demagogy combined with cynicism has already granted in Ireland, in Britain, in Holland, in Spain, in Denmark, in Norway, and that in Italy a law passed by the former leftist government granted for non-binding referendums. A right (or rather an alleged right) that the leftist presidents of various regions want to extend «at least» to local elections. A right (or an alleged right) that the Extreme Left wants to grant also to the irregulars. That is, to the illegal immigrants. Nor does it end here. Because the battle for granting them the right to vote and be elected in parliamentary elections has been taken up by the Party of Italian Communists which would like to reduce to three years the ten years of residence currently required to obtain citizenship.

But the worst is not even this. It is that such Crusade's Crusaders are not only in the Left and in the Extreme Left: they are on the opposite side as well, and in the so-called Center. At the Conference on Immigration organized by the European Union, the Deputy Prime Minister and leader of the Conservatives declared that «giving immigrants the vote is legitimate because immigrants pay their taxes (sic) and want to integrate». (Sic). On a visit to Cairo, the president of the European Commission added that giving the vote to immigrants with the Residence Card is «fundamental» in local elections and sooner or later it will have to be granted for electing the Parliament too. All things that drive me to speak about the other subtle and crawling way chosen by the Islamic community to penetrate the European society and take possession of it: the so-called Drafts of Agreement. I mean the Drafts that the sons of Allah demand to impose their habits and rules. Their way to eat in our schools and hospitals and prisons. Their way to dress and to pray in our streets and public places. Their way to marry, to rule the wife, to divorce her. Their way to work, to study, to die, to get buried...

So let's get to those Drafts.

CHAPTER 4

«Give him a fingernail and he'll take your hand. Give him a hand and he'll take your arm. Give him an arm and he will grab you by the neck to throw you out the window» my mother used to say when she didn't trust someone. And in some ways these Drafts of Agreement give the impression to ask not for a fingernail only but for a hand or, even better, an arm. Some requests are very astutely worded and play on ambiguity, but others immediately hurl you out of the window. Take the case of their Sunday which is not Sunday but Friday. «Muslims working for the State and for public or private enterprises, people who are engaged in independent or commercial business, people who serve in the Army or are assigned to other community service will and shall have the right to observe the Friday religious holiday» states the Draft written by the Islamic Religious Community in Italy. The one written by the Union of Islamic Communities and Organizations in Italy, more or less the same. And, with a special regard to schooling, both of them add: «In scheduling exam timetables, school authorities shall take the necessary measures to allow Muslim students to be examined on a day other than Friday».

Question Number One: what about the fact that in Italy and all over the West we take a break on Sunday, that the weekend includes Saturday, so Friday is a working day? I mean, what about the fact that the active week runs from Monday to Friday and no other religion has ever asked to reduce the active week from Monday to Thursday? Why should our school authorities alter their timetables to please the religious holiday of the Muslims? Question Number Two: what about the fact that adding Friday to the weekend alters the routine of our society and hurts its economy? What about the fact that State and public or private enterprises' employers involve railway workers, airline pilots, ambulance drivers, doctors, firefighters plus armed forces like those who perform police duties? I mean, what about the Carabiniere who at prayer time is arresting a thief? What about the doctor who at prayer time is performing a surgery? What about the ambulance driver who at prayer time is bringing an injured person to hospital? What about the pilot who at prayer time is taking off or landing, or the railway-worker who is driving a train, or the firefighter who is putting out a fire? In 1979 the daughters of Bazargan (Khomeini's Prime Minister) told me that one Friday, to beseech Allah at prayer time, daddy stopped on a Los Angeles freeway. Everybody knows: along the Los Angeles freeways the traffic is so intense that we cannot even slow down. Yet daddy stopped. He got out with his prayer mat, laid it on the asphalt, knelt on it, started praying and caused three accidents. Almost mortal. Better: in 1991, during the Gulf War, I saw a Saudi expert in explosive who together with two Marines was defusing an unexploded bomb. Well, all of a sudden he abandoned the delicate operation, regardless the Marines' protests left with the words «Sorry, it is my prayer time» and, while the two ran away with me, the bomb went off.

Among the apparently innocuous Drafts' demands there is also one concerning the work's interruption to recite the morning and the midday and the afternoon and the sunset Allah-akbars. There is also one concerning the celebration of Ramadan, the Hegirian New Year, the 10 of Dhul Hijjah of the Hegirian Calendar, and one concerning the supplementary holiday they want for the pilgrimage to Mecca. (All festivities they obviously add to our Christmas, New Year, Easter, Patron Saints, Immaculate Conceptions, May Firsts, etcetera). Finally, there's the matter of the identity papers' photo. And here we are. Article 3 of the Public Safety's Regulations' Text points out that identity papers must carry a photo where the holder appears bare-headed. That is, without a hat. Which is right, since a hat hides the hair and almost always the forehead and ears: three features which help to recognize an individual. In fact, when Italy was not an Islam colony, those features were indicated on passports along with the stature and the size and the eyes colour: remember? High or low forehead. Normal or protruding ears. Blond or black or gray or white hair, baldness... And nobody can deny that a turban hides the hair and the ears. The hijab too. Nobody can deny that along with the hair and the ears a chador hides the forehead as well as the temples, the cheekbones, the jaw, the chin and the neck. But the Drafts state that Muslim women can display documents where their photo shows a fully covered head. Covered with a chador or with a hijab. (With a turban, in the case of men). And too bad if this infringes the Public Safety's Law. I say «too bad» because, in 1995, the President of the Italian Supreme Court of Cassation issued a regulation, an ordinance, with which he informed the police authorities that the hat and the turban are a simple dress-accessory. As to the chador and the hijab, they are an integral part of Islamic dress. Then it concluded: «In order not to violate the constitutional principle guaranteed by Article 19 regarding worship and religious freedom, it is permitted to place on identity documents a photo with the head covered by such accessories and clothing».

(Letter to the President of the Italian Supreme Court of Cassation. «Illustrious Excellency. First of all, the hat is not a "simple accessory" or rather a frivolous and superfluous item. It is a garment that on winter protects the head from the cold and on summer shades it from the sun. Ever since Adam and Eve, most human beings have used it for these reasons. Secondly, the turban is certainly not an integral part of Islamic dress. In many Muslim countries you see it only on mullahs and imams' heads. In Turkey and in Egypt and in Morocco, for instance, men wear the fez. In Saudi Arabia and in Jordan and in Palestine etcetera, the keffiah. The turban is not a symbol of Islam. If you had done your homework you would have discovered that, far from defining it as an "Islamic garment", all dictionaries and encyclopaedias define it as "Oriental or women's head-dress". And the Orient, thank God, is not composed of Muslim countries only. It includes India, for instance, which despite Muslim invasions has always managed to remain Hindu. In India the turban was used a long time before Prophet Mohammed. Think of the black turban of the gurus, of the jewelled turban of the maharajas, of the red turban of the Sikhs who by the way are the most unbending enemies of Islam. The Assyrians used the turban too. The ancient Egyptians as well, starting with the Pharaohs and the Pharaohs wives. Nefertiti for instance. Besides, women have always used the turban. In every age and in every part of the world. When I was a child, my aunt Bianca wore one too. She said: "It's becoming". That being the case, Illustrious Excellency, I remind you that All-are-Equal-before-the-Law. And since all are equal before the law, I claim the right to put on my passport a photo with a hat. A broad-brimmed hat with the brim coming down over my forehead and throwing a shadow over my eyes. I claim this right and if it is not acknowledged I shall report you all for racial and religious discrimination. I shall take you to the Court of The Hague». End of the letter).

And now let's move to one of the most brazen demands contained in the Drafts. The one which wants to impose on us the validity of Islamic marriage.

* * *

There are two types of Islamic marriage. One is the classical marriage or *nikah*: a contract that falls under the «category of sales-transactions» and which, possible repudiation apart, has no time limit. The other is the temporary marriage or *mut'a*: a contract that falls under the category of «rents and leases» and may last any time. An hour, a week, a month. Or as much as mine lasted in 1979, when I went to interview Khomeini in the holy city of Qom and the mullah in charge of Morality Control compelled me to marry the interpreter already married to a jealous Spanish girl. (By the way: in *The Rage and the Pride* I told the hilarious story but I left it unfinished, and ever since I have been pursued by the question «But did you marry the jealous Spanish girl's husband or not?!?». Well, the answer is: yes, I did. You bet I did. On the spot. Or, rather, it was he who married me by signing the paper that the mullah waved while shouting «Shame-on-you, shame-on-you». He had caught us alone in the room, remember? A crime that in the case of an unmarried couple foresees the hanging or the firing-squad. Without that signature we both would have been executed, and good-bye interview with Khomeini. However that marriage, valid for only four months, never was consummated: I swear. As soon as completed the interview I left Iran with unadulterated virtue and thank God I never saw that temporary husband again).

Unlike the *nikah*, in fact, the *mut'a* is an expedient to legitimize casual sex. A pharisaical loophole to commit adultery without falling into sin, a trick to prostitute women. Not by chance, even the sons of Allah are embarrassed by it. The Sunnis have abolished it, the Shiites practise it on the quiet, and both prefer the *nikah*: classical marriage imposed by the two families in defiance of the spouses' wishes. (Which, if I'm not mistaken, is inadmissible under Italian law and the European Convention because both the one and the other require the betrothed's full and free consent). Oh no: the *nikah* does not give a damn about the feelings and wishes of the couple. No freedom of choice, no full consent: «Love deceives. Physical attraction, too. A marriage contract cannot be arranged on the foundation of love and the importance of physical attraction. The choice of partners must be based on the judgement of others» writes Islamic scholar Yusuf al-Qaradawi in his book *The Licit and the Illicit*. After the families have signed the contract and made and received payment of the *mahr*, that is, the money with which the groom purchases the bride, the betrothed don't even have the right to know each other and meet each other. If they meet by chance they must look at the floor or elsewhere, and woe betide their soul if they exchange a word. The bride cannot even speak during the ceremony. In fact she is not the one who says «I do». The «I do» is said for her by her *wali*, that is, her guardian: the man who conducted the negotiations. Usually, her father or brother. Because during the ceremony it is not she who stands beside the groom. It is her father or brother who looks into the groom's eyes, smiles sweetly at him, holds his hand. (I saw this scene, once. I saw it in a hotel in Islamabad, and it stunned me so that I concluded: «By Jove, this is a homosexual wedding!». Then, totally convinced of witnessing a homosexual wedding, I asked a guest whether the Koran allowed such practice. The guest was an uncle of the bride and I won't tell you how he answered...). «I give you this woman as required by the law of Allah and the Prophet» declares the father or brother of the bride. «I take this woman as required by the law of Allah and the Prophet» replies the groom. «You accept her, then?» the father or brother insists. «I already have» the groom replies. Then the groom and the father or brother of the bride exchange a kiss. A triple kiss. They wish each other best wishes, then say: «Let's hope she will prove to be a good wife». And while this is going on the bride remains in a corner, all silent. All alone and all silent. Which means «I do». Also her laughter, if she laughs, means «I do». Also her tears. If she weeps.

The second thing to say about the Islamic marriage is that in our society the polygamy is forbidden. «Marriage may not be contracted by anybody bound with a previous marriage» warns Article 86 of Italian Civil Code. And Article 556 of the Criminal Code adds: «Anybody who, though being bound by a valid marriage, contracts another marriage, will be punished up to five years of imprisonment. The same punishment will be applied to anybody who contracts a marriage with a person already married». Yet the Drafts of Agreement demand that «the Italian Republic recognize the validity of a marriage celebrated with Islamic rites». They demand that «the faculty of celebrating or dissolving marriages according to Islamic law and tradition remains intact also in the cases when such marriages have no civil validity or status». They demand it with the usual ambiguity, the usual guile. That is, without pointing out that Islamic marriage does not rule out bigamy. That at any time a husband may take another wife and then another and another up to four. They demand it, furthermore, without specifying whether by the word «marriages» (in the plural) they mean only *nikah* or *nikah* and *mut'a*. They demand it without clarifying whether by the word «dissolving» they refer to divorce or repudiation. And repudiation authorizes a husband to get rid of his wife whenever he feels like. To get rid of her, all he has to do is say one word three times: «Talak, talak, talak». They demand it, finally, without admitting that the term «Islamic tradition» means the total subjection of the wife. Her total slavery. And such slavery includes the husband's right to beat her, whip her, cane her, abuse her morally and physically. «Virtuous wives obey their husband unconditionally. Disobedient ones must be chased from his bed and caned» the Koran teaches. «Man is the undisputed Lord, the absolute Master, of the family. The woman may not rebel against his authority and, if she dares to do so, she must be beaten» adds al-Qaradawi in his book. (Printed in the year 2000, not 1000).

Al-Qaradawi also underlines that a wife may not leave the house if her husband does not permit it. She may not be visited by relatives and friends if he does not wish it. She may not have any part in the upbringing of their children if he does not authorize her to. In this regard the Federación Española de Entidades Religiosas Islámicas' Councillor, imam Mohammed Kamal Mustafa, has even written a *Wife-beating Handbook*. («Use a thin, light, and long cane. That is, good also for striking her from a distance. Strike her only on the body, the hands, the feet. Never on the face otherwise the scars and bruises will show. Don't forget that the blows must inflict also psychological suffering. Not only physical»). And the imam of Valencia,

Abdul Majad Rejab, has commented: «Imam Mustafa is Islamically correct. Wife-beating is a big resource». The imam of Barcelona, Abdelaziz Hazan, has added: «Imam Mustafa confines himself to reporting what is written in the Koran. If he didn't, he would be a heretic». The fact is that, like any other European yet Western Constitution, the Italian Constitution establishes total equality between husband and wife. It defends women's freedoms, it forbids any act of discrimination against them, it lays down that spouses enjoy equal rights and have equal duties. It also states that, either during marriage either after a possible divorce, they have equal responsibilities towards their children. Ergo, legal recognition of Islamic marriage is for us impossible. Inconceivable. Inadmissible. Equally impossible and inconceivable and inadmissible, the demand to define Islam as «the second State religion of Italy». A demand that those Drafts put forth in order to exact the teaching of the Koran in our schools. Here's why.

* * *

The secularism of our State schools is not perfect. It is not because of the Lateran Pacts, the Concordat that Mussolini signed with the Vatican in 1929 and that the Constituent Assembly upheld in 1947 with the votes of the Communists led by Togliatti. It is not because in 1984 it was modified only with the abrogation of the unconstitutional term «State Religion» and, relying on the fact that the overwhelming majority of Italians is Catholic, left a small blemish named «weekly hour of religion». An optional hour, though. So optional that it was optional even when I was an ultra-radical student at the Classical Lyceum «Galileo Galilei» of Florence and I drove to despair an adorable priest named don Bensi. When don Bensi entered the classroom, in fact, I used to leave. Deaf to his saddened comments, (usually a mumbled «Off-you-go, off-you-go! Never-say-that-a-poor-priest-tries-to-save-your-rotten-soul»), I picked up my snack and went to eat it in the corridor. Without risking any vendetta or punishment, mind that. Even less from him who at my return in the classroom forgave me with a tender and ironical chuckling: «Was it a good snack?». I mean: the possibility of choosing, of accepting or rejecting that hour, strongly minimizes the small blemish.

It minimizes it to such an extent that no other religious community objects to it. No other religious community expects its doctrine to be taught in our State schools. Not even the Jewish one which among all the religious minorities is the most devoted to its confession. The most demanding. In its Agreement with the Italian Republic the Jewish Community speaks, yes, of «possible requests that may come from pupils or from their families to start up a study of Judaism in the sphere of cultural activities». But proposing the-study-of-Judaism-in-the-sphere-of-cultural-activities is one thing, and teaching it in the lesson-hours is another. As a consequence, not only defining Islam as «the second State religion of Italy» is a gross stupidity by reason of the fact that Italians converted to Islam are a few thousands. Thus, much less than those belonging to the Jewish or to the Protestant religions. Not only that statement is ridiculous on account of the fact that the Italian State has not to represent and does not represent Muslim immigrants. But pretending to teach the Koran in our State schools is as unlawful as disrespectful to our secularism. And yet they demand it unambiguously, this time. Yet they demand so. They do it by specifying that Islam lessons must be carried out in classes of all types and levels. Kindergartens included. They do it by underlining that each lesson must be performed by teachers selected by an imam, with curricula written by an imam, and at hours of their own choice. Worse: they demand it by sticking their noses into our school curricula, and daring ask that «other religious principles be not spread through other subjects». And for Christsake, do you know what this means?!? It means that in the curricula of the «other-subjects» we should avoid any reference to the religion in which our culture is steeped. That is, Christianity. It means that in literature courses we should not include, for example, Dante Alighieri's *Divine Comedy*. A poem written by an infidel-dog who had an extremely different vision of earthly and non-earthly life. A Catholic who in the twenty-eighth Canto of the Inferno places the Prophet among the worst sinners. A Christian who fills Paradise with holy or virtuous women. Among them, his adored Beatrice Portinari. And, at the top of apotheosis, the «Daughter of her Son»: the Virgin Mary.

Literature courses should not either include, as a consequence, St. Francis' *Canticle of the Creatures* and Alessandro Manzoni's *Sacred Hymns*. History courses should not speak of Jesus nor of his Apostles. Nor of Barabbas and Pontius Pilate. Nor of the Christians and of their Catacombs. Nor of Constantine and of the Holy Roman Empire. They should also eliminate the struggles between the Guelphs and the Ghibellines, the resistance put up by the Sicilians and the Romans and the Campanians and the Tuscans and the Venetians and the Friulans and the Apulians and the Genovese to the Islamic invasions. They should remain silent on Charles Martel and Joan of Arc, on the fall of Constantinople and on the battle of Lepanto. Philosophy courses should cancel the works of Saint Augustine and Thomas Aquinas, of Luther and Calvin, of Descartes and Pascal etcetera. History of Art courses should ignore all the Christs and the Madonnas of Giotto and Masaccio, of Beato Angelico and Filippino Lippi, of Verrocchio and Mantegna, of Raffaello and Leonardo da Vinci and Michelangelo. Music should eliminate all the Gregorian chants, all the Requiems starting with Mozart's and Haydn's and Verdi's *Requiem*, and woe betide the teacher who asks to sing Schubert's *Ave Maria*.

These cases sound like paradoxes, don't they? They sound like jokes, exaggerations. But they are not. They are conclusions based on the reality we are living in. Indeed our invaders have already tried to censor our culture, have already pilloried some of its infidel-dogs. Listen to me, listen: one is Dante Alighieri who on the pretext of the twenty-eighth Canto of the Inferno, the Canto where the Prophet burns, should be banned from high schools as well as evicted from his tomb in Ravenna where his bones should be «smashed and scattered to the wind». Another one is Giovanni da Modena who in 1415, in the cathedral of

San Petronio of Bologna, painted a tiny fresco portraying the Prophet as above. They even sent the Pope and the Cardinals a letter in which the tiny fresco is described as «an unacceptable insult to Muslims of the whole world». Better: they promised to destroy it and once they tried. More or less, what they do in France when they ask to ban Voltaire. Guilty, poor guy, of having written *Le Fanatisme ou Mahomet le prophète*: a tragedy in which, at Mohammed's instigation, the young protagonist kills his father and his brother who are infidel-dogs.

As for the demands I have not mentioned as yet, well... The tamest is the one concerning refectories in every public or private company, in every prison and every hospital, every military barracks and every school should serve also Islamic food. Meaning no pork and, at its place, halal meat. But this is a practically useless request, given the fact that most refectories already apply it. In each prison (in our prisons most of the inmates are Algerians or Moroccans or Tunisians or Albanians or Sudanese or Rumanians) halal meat has replaced the one from our slaughterhouses. Pork has virtually disappeared, and by the way: who stands to make money out of this halal meat business? Only the pious throat-cutters of Turin or also Islamic mafia, a mafia similar to the one that with the halal meat triumphs in France? The most unpleasant demand, instead, concerns the burial of their dead. Which, according to Islamic rite, must take place barely below ground and with the body wrapped in a simple sheet. No coffin. (Something which in Italy is strictly prohibited by Health Regulations). Anyway the most loathsome demand in my opinion is the one which exacts «full collaboration in the protection of the historical, artistic, environmental, architectural, archeological, archive, library heritage of Islamism. This, for the purpose of facilitating the collection and reordering of Islamic cultural assets».

The most loathsome, yes. Because what are the Islamic-cultural-assets you speak about, you shameless rascals?!? What historical and artistic and environmental and architectural and archeological and archive library heritage of Islamism, you impudent vultures?!? Also in my country your ancestors brought nothing but the cry «Mamma, the Turks!». They left nothing but the tears of creatures whom your pirates killed or raped or abducted to fill the slave markets in Cairo, in Tunis, in Algiers, in Rabat, in Istanbul. The women and the newborn babies to be sold in the harems possessed by sultans and viziers and sheikhs sick with sex and paedophilia. The men, to slaughter or to break in your stone quarries. The boys and the youths, to be turned into fighting machines. From Mazzara to Syracuse, from Syracuse to Taranto, from Taranto to Bari, from Bari to Ancona, from Ancona to Ravenna, from Ravenna to Udine, from Genova to Livorno, from Livorno to Pisa, from Pisa to Rome, from Rome to Salerno, from Salerno to Palermo, Muslims always came only to take. Only to plunder. So in our museums, our archives, our libraries, among our archeological and architectural treasures, there is not a damn thing that belongs to you. But do we really need the brazen-faced Drafts of Agreement to conclude that those eternal invaders rule us already?

To answer this question all we need is knowing the case that in the last three years has been afflicting Tuscany. For almost half a century, a feud of the Communists and consequently a stronghold of the sons of Allah. I mean, the case of Colle Val d'Elsa: the medieval town that Dante Alighieri mentions in the thirteenth Canto of Purgatory and which, blessed by one of the finest Chianti landscapes, lies ten miles from Siena. Because on the top of its hill, a hill that seems to have been painted by Duccio Boninsegna or Simone Martini or Ambrogio Lorenzetti, the Center-Left Council wants to erect a mosque comparable to the grand mosque of Rome. That's right. A grand, a grandiose mosque with dome and courtyard and palms, completed by an eighty-feet-high minaret and embellished by the buildings of the new Islamic Center that the local Muslims demand. Listen to me, listen.

* * *

It all began a month after September 11, when the rubbles of the Twin Towers were still smoking but a press-agency communiqué informed the world that the leftist mayor of Colle Val d'Elsa had allocated a billion and a half liras (around a million dollars) to expand on public land the Islamic Center and transfer it to an area capable of accommodating the mosque. A mosque enriched by the over-mentioned minaret of which the Muslim Community of Siena and Province was in the most pressing need. With the mosque, three hundred and fifty residence units that the community needed as much. With the residence units, an Islamic cemetery in perpetual property. All things of which the twenty thousand citizens of Colle Val d'Elsa knew absolutely nothing and had not consequently expressed any opinion, given no approval.

Well, the hell broke loose. Blasphemous yellings. Slanging matches. Appeals to the Court of Justice. As well as furious debates and petitions to halt the triple project. The mayor had no right to give away public land and spend public money on enterprises which favoured foreigners and damaged citizens, people said. Besides, how did the mayor dare to build a mosque enriched by a minaret in an environment that with mosques and minarets had nothing to do?!? There were only three hundred Muslims at Colle Val d'Elsa and one thousand in the province of Siena: so where was the «pressing need»? As for the cemetery, the municipal one was open to the deceased of any creed. Why did the Muslims had to have their own personal one, their own special one? Why should their tombs be in perpetuity while the Christians and the Jews and the Buddhists and the atheists were kept in their graves for no longer than a few decades? A Defence Committee was also formed. «Stop the mosque, stop the cemetery! Hands off our land!». A committee composed of labour-workers, farmers, pensioners, housewives. Usually, people who had voted for the Left. But it achieved nothing. And soon the mosque with the minaret will disfigure the landscape of Duccio Boninsegna and Simone Martini and Ambrogio Lorenzetti. A mosque with a minaret as high as ninety feet. And, as if it were not enough, another one will raise in Florence where the jealous and leftist administration has decided to rival Colle Val d'Elsa inside the historical center of the city. Meaning into the homeland of Dante Alighieri, of Petrarca, Boccaccio, Giotto, Michelangelo, Leonardo da Vinci, Lorenzo il Magnifico. And so on and so on... In fact now I ask myself through what negligence or stupidity or destiny people like me failed to realize in time that we were coming to this. And while I ask it, my memory goes back to the Sixties. It takes me back to May 1966 when in Miami, Florida, I interviewed a boxer born with the name of Cassius Clay but, through his conversion to Islam, had become Muhammad Ali.

CHAPTER 5

It takes me back because that interview should have opened my eyes. Or, in the least, should have led me to suspect that in the West something very very dangerous was going on. Prospectively, more dangerous than the Cold War: the nightmare we were living through at that time. In the Sixties, in fact, an unprecedented wave of Islamic students from Muslim Africa, financed by Arab countries, invaded both Europe and the United States with the slogan «Revival of Islam». And especially in the United States a sect known as the «Nation of Islam» or «Black Muslims Movement» unleashed a bellicose campaign of proselytism. Mosques were built in New York, Boston, Philadelphia, Chicago, Detroit, Atlanta, Denver, Los Angeles, San Francisco. And although the majority of the black population identified with Baptist minister Martin Luther King, a good number of Afro-Americans became followers of the Prophet. Black Muslims, to be precise. Oh, I remember them well, the Black Muslims. They weren't very likeable. Without anybody denouncing them for racism they stood for the absolute superiority of the black race and the consequent inferiority of the white race. For the whites they nourished a ferocious hate, for Martin Luther King a contempt which reached the infamy of calling him «Uncle Tom» or «boiled fish», and they were led by a man who made no secret of his intentions: Elijah Muhammad born Eliah Poole. «Convert, convert, convert. Brothers, soon we will have to convert the white devils too. Conversion will be an absolute necessity because only by liberating the United States can we liberate Europe, meaning the entire West» said Elijah Muhammad born Eliah Poole. Until 1965 there was also the controversial character who had converted to Islam in the penitentiary where he was serving a long sentence for burglary: Malcolm X born Malcolm Little. That Malcolm X whom the young of today know only through the sanctification accorded to his memory by a famous Hollywood movie. That Malcolm X who in 1963 commented on the assassination of John Kennedy with the words «they've-roasted-the-chicken». And who seized by a sudden attack of mysticism in 1964 embraced the idea of brotherhood but the following year was gunned down by his disciples. So that his place went to Louis Abdul Farrakhan born Louis Eugene Walcott: the calypso singer whose racist ravings were summed up by the following words: «The inferiority of the white race and of the Christian religion is proved by the fact that all human progress has been achieved by Islam. The only white man worthy of respect is Adolf Hilter, my idol also because he tried to get us rid of the Jews». The star of the moment, meanwhile, was a young boxer called Muhammad Ali born Cassius Clay: holder of the world heavyweight title.

I used to judge him a freak of nature, Muhammad Ali born Cassius Clay. So at that time I didn't take him seriously, I didn't see him as a danger. How can you see a danger in a guy who says: «I am the greatest and the most good-looking. I'm so good-looking that I deserve three women a night. I'm so great that only Allah can knock me out». Or: «I chose the name Muhammad because Muhammad means Worthy of All Praise, and indeed I am a man worthy of all praise». Or: «Have I ever written a letter, read a book? Certainly not. I don't write letters. I don't read books. I don't because I know more than you all. I even know that Allah is an older God than your Jehovah and your Jesus, and that the Arabic is a language much older than English. In fact English is only four hundred years old». Or: «What will I do after I stop boxing? Well, maybe I'll become head of an African State which needs a supreme leader and asks itself: why don't we take Muhammad Ali who's so strong and good-looking and brave and religious?». Or: «If I lived in Alabama instead of Florida, I would vote for those who don't mix whites with blacks. Not for guys like Sammy Davis who marry Swedish blonde girls. Dogs must stay with dogs, lice must stay with lice, whites must stay with whites». In other words, I saw no threat in that caricature of stupidity and nastiness. That parody of evil. Yet a couple of times I was seized by doubt. By the thought that not taking him seriously was a mistake, that his case might be more significant than it seemed. The first time, (we met twice), when he said to me: «I love Elijah Muhammad much more than my mother. Because Elijah Muhammad is a Muslim and my mother is a Christian. I could even die for Elijah Muhammad. For my mother, not at all». The second time when the Black Muslims crowding his house assaulted me because I had sent him to Hell. He was very hostile, that day. Very resentful and particularly nasty. Instead of answering my questions he snorted, scratched himself, ate massive slices of watermelon and belched in my face. (Deliberately, by the way. To offend me. To remind me that dogs must stay with dogs, lice with lice, whites with whites. Not to digest better). Belches so cyclopean, so blaring, so smelly, that in the end my patience ran out. I threw the recorder microphone, stood up, and articulating a well-deserved «Go to Hell» I walked out. I went to the taxi waiting for me in front of his house. Well, at first he showed no reaction. Struck with astonishment he sat with a slice of watermelon in mid-air and didn't even have the impulse to flatten me with one of his deadly knock-out punches. But the Black Muslims came after me. Led by his Spiritual Advisor (a certain Sam Saxon) they reached the taxi I had just rejoined, and shouting «filthy Christian» they surrounded it. They started lifting it, trying to overturn it, and... The street was deserted. The terrified driver (a black man wearing a necklace with a Coptic cross) couldn't get the engine start, couldn't drive away. And if a police car hadn't happened to pass by (a miracle that seriously put my religious unbelief at stake) I wouldn't be here to tell the story.

The thought that not taking him seriously could be a mistake also occurred to me when I heard that thanks to him Islamic proselytism had increased a lot. (And don't forget that today, in America, eighty-five percent of Muslims are black. Don't forget that blacks are converting at the rate of one hundred thousand a year and that many come from the world of sport. For instance, the once heavyweight champion Malik Abdul

Aziz born Mike Tyson: the one who during the fights bites or rather eats his opponents' ears. For instance, the basketball champion Kareem Abdul-Jabbar born Lew Alcindor. Or Mahmoud Abdul-Rauf born Chris Jackson, also a basketball champion. And recently they have landed big fish in showbusiness too. Denzel Washington, the Oscar-winner who played Malcolm X, for a start. And, it seems, Michael Jackson: the multi-millionaire jester who likes to sleep with little boys and who in order to cancel his African look subjected himself to such cruel plastic surgery that his features are no longer those of a black male. They are those of a noseless white girl). But I pushed those thoughts away. I dismissed them by telling myself that the Black Muslims were fruit of a society where religious obsession produces continuous surprises. Wasn't it America that spawned the Mormons of the Church-of-Jesus-Christ-of-the-Latter-Day-Saints, that is the followers of that Joseph Smith who preached unlimited polygamy and had no fewer than fifty-four wives? Wasn't it America that spawned the Jehovah's Witnesses, that is the followers of that Charles Taze Russell who taught to spit on the US flag and on the crucifix? Wasn't it America that spawned the Christian Scientists, that is the followers of Mary Baker Eddy who in the Bible saw the cure for all diseases and woe betide you if you call the doctor or get hospitalized or take an aspirin? Wasn't it America that spawned the perverts of the Church of Satan, meaning the followers of Anton LaVey who in Satan saw the source of any redemption? I even concluded that the African students entering the universities to spread propaganda for the Revival of Islam were a passing phase: the temporary phenomenon of a migratory flow similar to the one of the Cubans and the Mexicans. And, deceived by such thinking, I failed to realize that the same phenomenon was affecting Europe.

To begin with, Britain: the country where the Revival of Islam came from Pakistan, Uganda, Nigeria, Sudan, Kenya, Tanzania. Then, France: the country where it came from Algeria, Tunisia, Morocco, Mauritania, Chad, Cameroon. Then, Belgium: the country where it came from Congo and Burundi. Then, Holland: the country where it came from Indonesia and Surinam and Moluccas. Then, Italy: the country where it came from Libya, Somalia, Eritrea. (That year the University for Foreigners in Perugia was overflowing with the Libyan students who had founded the Muslim Students' Union and were preparing to build Italy's first mosque). What I did not understand is that, far from being a normal migratory flow, this phenomenon was part of a specific strategy. Meaning a design based on gradual penetration rather than brutal and sudden aggression against the infidel-dogs and infidel-bitches of the planet. Even less I realized that in those years, the Sixties, the Revival of Islam was spreading also in the Soviet Union. Specifically in Kazakhstan, in Kyrgyzstan, in Turkmenistan, in Uzbekistan, in Tajikistan, in the regions once conquered by the Golden Horde. And in the heart of Russia itself. That is, in the Autonomous Territory of the Chechens. Those Chechens with whom at the end of the 1700s Catherine the Great had been forced to deal, and against whom in the 1800s the Tsars had fought for forty-seven years. Those Chechens that only Tsar Alexander the II would have been able, in 1859, to halt.

* * *

A few did realize the danger, I know. If you consult the library you find many essays on the subject. But most of them went unobserved, un-listened. The Cold War sucked everything. I mean: most of my generation did not care about Islamism, did not worry for the term Revival of Islam. At that time we only spoke about Communism. Socialism, Marxism, Leninism, Bolshevism, Cold War. Besides, the Cold War included the war in Vietnam, and the war in Vietnam was escalating desperately. In April 1966 the B52s bombed Hanoi for the first time, and in Saigon the Vietcong responded with a massacre at Tan Son Nhut airport. In May the Buddhists began to roast themselves at the rate of two monks or two nuns a day, and the North Vietnamese infiltrating the South reached the 90.000 units. The American troops, 300.000. They would soon reach a total of half a million. Thus...

The other night I went on a journey back into that past and, as if to reproach myself for failing to understand, I looked for clues similar to those of the Watermelon Eater. But I found none. In 1967 and 1968 and 1969, I was in Vietnam. North and South. In 1970, in Cambodia. And instead of minarets, instead of mosques and burkas and djellabahs and chadors, my memory called up the streets of Saigon. The paddy fields of the Mekong Delta. The forests of the Central Highlands. The dead in uniform and without uniform. Instead of the wails of the muezzins it called up the throb of the helicopters and the rattle of machine-guns. The thud of shellfire. The whistle of the rockets, the moans of the wounded soldiers calling out for their mothers in English and in Vietnamese. «Mommy, mommy». «Mama, mama». I saw myself in Dak

To, in My Tho, in Da Nang, in Na Trang, in Tri Quang, in Kontum, in Quang Ngai, in Phu Bai, in Hué, in Hanoi, in Saigon where one day of 1968 three French journalists came from Paris. In those days, the stronghold of the so-called Sixty-Eighters: the wordmongers skilled in the art of wall-daubing. They came and turning to the Vietnamese employee who took care of the Agence France Press' telex, one of them pompously harangued: «Vous ne savez pas ce qu'il se passe à Paris, mon vieux. You don't know what's happening in Paris, old chap». But the Vietnamese looked at him with contemptuous melancoly and answered: «Vous ne savez pas ce qu'il se passe ici, you don't know what's happening here, Monsieur». (What was happening was the May Offensive, the bloody battle of Hué, the tragic siege of Khe Sanh. The aftermath of the Tet Offensive).

Rummaging through 1968 I also saw myself in Memphis, Tennessee, where Martin Luther King had just been assassinated. I also saw myself in Los Angeles where Bobby Kennedy had been assassinated as well. I also saw myself in Mexico City, that is in the massacre of Plaza Tlatelolco, then in the morgue where I had ended up with the corpses. All places where you didn't see the minarets and mosques, you didn't hear wails of muezzins. (Though Bob Kennedy had been killed by a

Muslim Arab: remember? A detail that nobody ever points out). In 1969 there was the first episode of Islamic terrorism, the aircraft hijacked at Fiumicino by Mrs. Leila Khaled and blown up in Damascus: true. But in 1969 I was in Hanoi, I was in South Vietnam's Son Tay, Hoa Binh, Ninh Binh, Thanh Hoa. In 1970 Islamic terrorism erupted in full: equally true. A Swissair plane blew up in mid-air with forty-eight passengers and the five hijacked aircraft blew up too. Moreover, anti-Semitism re-emerged. An anti-Semitism of which the pro-Arab Left immediately made itself the standard-bearer. With the re-emergence of anti-Semitism, the brainwashing of people in good faith. «Poor-Palestinians, they're-forced-to-kill-us, aren't-they? All Israel's fault». But in 1970 I was in Cambodia's Svai Rieng, Prei Veng, Kompong Cham, Tang Krasang, Roca Kong, Phnom Penh. The Vietnam war had spread to Cambodia where in combat the mommy-mommy or the mama-mama moans deafened me even more than in Vietnam. And, here too, no Revival of Islam.

Listen, the world I had glimpsed in Miami with Cassius Clay-Muhammad Ali and his Black Muslims reappeared to me only in 1971. That is, when I went to Bangladesh to cover the Indo-Pakistan war and in Dacca I saw the slaughter that I speak about in *The Rage and the Pride*. (I also saw the cement-quarry where a couple of days earlier the Muslims had massacred eight hundred Hindus. Many women included. And where their corpses lay abandoned to the appetite of the vultures. Hundreds and hundreds of vultures unrolling long paper-streamers which were not paper-streamers: they were the Hindu bowels torn out by their beaks and carried up in the sky). Yes, I rediscovered that world in Dacca. But I didn't analyze it until 1972 when, to understand the Palestinians-forced-to-kill-us, I went to the country they had invaded like they would later invade Lebanon: Jordan. Here I visited the secret bases from which they left to attack the kibbutzes and witnessed the arrogance with which they swaggered Amman, the brutality with which they broke in the foreigners' hotels and requested money at kalashnikov-point. Here I interviewed the nephew of Amin al-Husseini, I mean the former Grand Mufti of Jerusalem who at Nuremberg had been tried by default for his collaborationism with Nazi Germany. Who in 1944 had gone to Berlin to pay homage to Hitler. Who shouting Death-to-Tito-friend-of-the-Jews-and-enemy-of-Mohammed had played godfather to the «Handzar Trennung», the Islamic SS Division of twenty-one thousand Bosnians. And who, protected by the Palestinians, was now hiding in Beirut.

It was Mr. Yasser Arafat, the nephew of so much uncle. And, as I tell elsewhere, my interview with him fully demonstrated that genetic heredity is not a matter of opinion. But this did not open my eyes, as yet. Arafat was too half-witted to open anything. The enlightment came in Beirut when I interviewed his rival George Habash: the man who carried out the bloodiest terrorists' attacks in Europe. His rival. Because, while a conscientious bodyguard protected him by pointing his sub-machine gun at my head, with absolute clarity Habash explained to me that the Arabs' enemy was not Israel alone: it was the whole West. America, Europe: the West. Among the targets to hit he cited in fact Italy, France, Germany, Switzerland. And now read carefully, please, don't miss a word of what he said. «Our revolution is a part of the world revolution. It is not confined to the reconquest of Palestine» he said. «The time has come to admit that we want a war like the war in Vietnam. That we want another Vietnam, and not only for Palestine but for all the Arab countries». Then he said: «The Palestinian problem is not an aside problem. A problem separated from the Arab Nation's realities. Palestinians are *part* of the Arab Nation. Therefore the entire Arab Nation must go to war against Europe and America. It must unleash a war against the West. And it will. America and Europe don't know that we Arabs are just at the beginning of the beginning. That the best has yet to come. That from now on there will be no peace for the West». Finally he said: «To advance step by step. Millimetre by millimetre. Year after year. Decade after decade. Determined, stubborn, patient. This is our strategy. A strategy that we shall expand throughout the whole planet».

*   *   *

Oh yes, my eyes opened because of George Habash. The trouble is that they didn't open completely, and know why? Because (mea culpa-mea culpa) I believed that Habash referred only to the terrorist attacks, to the massacres. I didn't understand that talking about the war on the West, about the-strategy-to-be-expanded, he did not mean the war waged with weapons and that's all. He also meant the cultural war, the demographic war, the religious war waged by stealing a country from its citizens. Step by step, millimetre by millimetre. Year after year. Decade after decade. Determinedly, stubbornly, patiently. In short, the war waged through immigration, fertility, presumed pluriculturalism, Drafts of Agreement's demands. The Islamic holidays, the five prayers' interruptions, the halal meat, the face covered also on the identity papers, to begin with. The Islamic marriage, the polygamy, the stoning of women, the assets to remove from the museums and from the archives and from the libraries, to go on...

Perhaps I didn't understand it because of the too many tragedies which that year hit us. The interview with Habash had taken place in mid-March, and on May 30 there was the assault by a suicide squad at the Lod airport. On August 4, the oil pipeline sabotage in Trieste. On August 16, the episode of the two British female tourists who in Rome had boarded a flight for Tel Aviv bringing along with them the tape-recorder received as a gift by Arab suitors. (The tape-recorder packed with TNT). On September 5, the attack at the Olympic Games of Munich with the death of eleven Israeli athletes... That those infamies were not the only face of the strategy mentioned by Habash became clear to me only in October 1973, when Syria and Egypt attacked Israel. I mean when the Yom Kippur or Ramadan War broke out and, at the same time, the OPEC countries imposed the oil embargo. It became even clearer in 1974, when during an interview the then Italian Minister of the Defense, Giulio Andreotti, told me about Those-Who-Drink-Orange-Juice. «Yes, now we also have the problem of those who drink orange juice».

«And who are those-who-drink-orange-juice?» I asked. «The Muslims, of course». «And what do the Muslims want?» I insisted. «A grand mosque in Rome».*

Then he explained that four months prior to the oil embargo His Majesty Faisal king of Saudi Arabia had come to Rome and here, drowning in rivers of orange juice, had met the President of the Italian Republic to express the wish of building a grandiose mosque in the capital of Christianity. «A grandiose mosque?!?» I shouted not understanding why the then few Muslims of Rome needed it. «Ah...!» Andreotti sighed in a sybilline way. «But the President of the Republic didn't

* *Note of the Author*. Notoriously a sincere friend of dictator Gaddafi and a warm admirer of Khomeini (two guys with whom he used to mantain privileged rapports), as a consequence the inspirator/instigator of pro-Arab policy and the protagonist of the most obscure seasons of Italian miseries, the ultra-Catholic but philo-leftist Giulio Andreotti has always been on the side of the Arabs. Of the Muslims, of the invaders. Recently he spanked me on the buttocks because of the golden medal I had been granted by the Regional Assembly of Tuscany for cultural and professional merits. He accused me of having ignited the frontal crash of the two civilizations and of advocating military solutions against the Islamic world. My suspicion is that, despite his familiarity with a couple of dead Popes, he cares much more for the Koran than he does for the Gospels.

agree, did he?». «Ah...!» Andreotti sighed in the same way. «And what does the Pope think about this?!?». «Ah!» Andreotti sighed again. The Pope was Giovanni Battista Montini: Paul VI. Certainly not a man who could be pleased by such a request. And I said it. I also said that it was the Prophet Mohammed who saw in the capital of Christianity the future capital of Islam. But again Andreotti went on with the sybilline sighing and did not even clarify whether he was in favour of it or not. So I left with the feeling that something irremediable was about to come. Something that had to do with the words of Habash, and of which the mosque in Rome was only the symbol. The archetype.

What happened in the following twenty years confirmed that feeling till the borders of a nightmare. Because rather soon the Mayor of Rome donated seven acres of public land to build the mosque and the Islamic Center which the few Muslims living at that time in Rome did not need at all. In order to express the glory of Islam, the Italian architect designed the project with a minaret eighty meters high. That is, twice as high as the highest domes and bell-towers of Rome. And, all excited by such a primacy, the whole of the Muslim countries decided to support the construction expenses. Saudi Arabia, Egypt, Lybia, Tunisia, Morocco, Algeria, Jordan, Yemen, Kuwait, Malaysia, Indonesia, Bangladesh, Senegal, Mauritania, Bahrain, the Sultanate of Oman, the United Arab Emirates... In 1984 the construction began and, as the grandiose building grew up, the number of Those-Who-Drink-Orange-Juice grew with it. When in 1995 the works were over and the solemn inauguration took place, its hypostyle hall and courtyard were not enough to hold all of them. The shoes and sandals left outside covered the entire perimeter of the seven acres. And by that time the same initiative had completed also the grand mosque of Paris, the grand mosque of Brussels, the grand mosque of Marseilles, plus the grand and small mosques of London, of Birmingham, of Bradford, of Cologne, of Hamburg, Strasbourg, Vienna, Copenhagen, Oslo, Stockholm, Madrid, Barcelona. And in Andalusia the grand mosque of Granada was being erected. In Kazakhstan, in Kyrgyzstan, in Turkmenistan, in Uzbekistan, in Tajikistan, mosques sprang up like mushrooms. Hence, the time has come to give a precise answer to the question I have left pending: how did we come to all this? What there is behind all this?

CHAPTER 6

There is the biggest conspiracy that modern history has created, behind all that. The most squalid plot that through ideological fraud, cultural indecency, moral prostitution, deception, our time has produced. A conspiracy, a plot, made possible by the bankers who invented the farce of the European Union. By the collaborationists and better yet the traitors who invented the lie of Pacifism. By the hypocrites who invented the fraud of Humanitarianism. By the heads of State who do not even comprehend the concept of State. By the politicians who do not even understand the concept of politics. By the intellectuals who do not even ponder about the concept of intellect. There is the lack of honour and dignity and conscience which characterize a society ill with lack of courage. There is also a Church, the Catholic Church, which for the moment seems to be uncapable of defending Christianity. And, above all, there is a Europe which does not know where it goes. Which has lost its identity and sold itself to the sultans, the caliphs, the viziers, the mercenaries of the new Ottoman Empire. In short, what I call Eurabia. And now I'll prove it with facts.

No, it is not mine this terrifying term Eurabia. It is not I who conceived this atrocious neologism which derives from the symbiosis of the words Europe and Arabia. *Eurabia* is the name of the little journal founded in 1975 by the official perpetrators of the plot, of the conspiracy: the Association France-Pays Arabes in Paris, the Middle East International Group in London, the Groupe d'Études sur le Moyen Orient in Geneva, and the European Coordinating Commitee of the Associations for Friendship with the Arab World. A trickery, the latter one, specially constituted by what at that time was called the EEC: European Economic Community. And which is now called the European Union.

It is not mine either the evidence that I am about to provide. Almost all of it comes from the extraordinary research which Bat Ye'or, renowned expert on Islam and author of books like *Islam and Dhimmitude*. (Dhimmitude means submission, servitude, to Allah. And Bat Ye'or means Daughter of the Nile). «If only I could prove that this time too Troy burns because the collaborationists, the traitors, really opened the doors and let the enemy in!» one day I said to her explaining that for them now I adopted the word «collaborationists», the traitors. And Bat Ye'Or replied: «That's easy». Then she sent me excerpts of her research, and reading them was like taking the lid off a saucepan whose contents were unknown to you but whose horrible smells were familiar. The research told in fact all the irresponsibilities and the aberrations that the nine countries of the European Economic Community had committed in the Seventies. The France of the Gaullist Pompidou, a France intoxicated by its longing to Napoleonize Europe, to start with. The Germany of Social-Democrat Willy Brandt, a Germany cut in half by the Wall, but back on its feet thus ready to impose again its diktats. And behind those two, holding their trail, the bit-part players, the extras. Then the vassals. Among the bit-part players, the extras, a decayed and enfeebled Britain unable to retain its leading role, plus a quarrelsome and pseudo-socialist Ireland that wasn't worth a fig but behaved as though it were worthy a jewel. Among the vassals, a Left-leaning Holland, a Denmark inward-looking and confused, a Luxembourg despicably docile and culturally smaller than its tiny surface area, a Belgium eternally at the heel of maman-la-France. And an Italy poisoned by the Socialist-Communists but at the same time enslaved by the Christian Democrat domination. Puppet-master of the horrendous binomial that soon would celebrate the marriage called Historic Compromise, the pro-Arab and super-Catholic Giulio Andreotti who had not yet promised the grandiose mosque to Those-Who-Drink-Orange-Juice but who drank as much orange juice as the leftists in love with Arafat. Not at random it was he who acted as godfather to the Italo-Libyan bank called UBAE: Arab-European Union Bank. It was he who fornicated with Gaddafi. And now let's see what Bat Ye'or research says.

It says that to fertilize the ovule of the plot, of the conspiracy, was the spermatozoon (Bat Ye'or calls it the trigger, detonator) of October 16th and 17th 1973. That is, the Conference which during the Yom Kippur War (or Ramadan War) the representatives of Saudi Arabia, Kuwait, Iran, Iraq, Qatar, Abu Dhabi, Bahrain, Algeria, Libya, (that is OPEC), held in Kuwait City where ipso facto the oil price quadrupled. From two dollars and 46 cents a barrel, to nine dollars and 60 cents. Refined oil, up to ten dollars and 46 cents. The OPEC representatives also announced that they would reduce the extraction of crude by 5 percent a month, that they would put an embargo on exports to the United States as well as to Denmark and Holland. Then they extended the embargo to anybody who would reject or fail to support their political demands. What demands? Israel's withdrawal from the occupied territories, recognition of the Palestinians, PLO presence at all peace negotiations, application of the principle expressed by UN Resolution 242. (The one that, based on the one-way pacifism, bans the acquisition of territory by means of war). However nineteen days later European Economic Community met in Brussels and signed a document proclaiming that Israel should abandon the occupied territories, that the PLO and Arafat should take part in peace negotiations, that the principle contained in Resolution 242 was sacrosanct. And on November 26 the couple Pompidou-Brandt had the most intimate tête-à-tête that France and Germany had enjoyed since Vichy. Better yet, since Napoleon married Marie Louise. Struck by panic, both decided that a summit-meeting was required to initiate talks with the Arab world and together lay down the foundations for a solid friendship with the Arab League. Then they informed their European counterparts and, starting with the Italians, all the counterparts agreed. In fact the Euro-Arab Dialogue opened with the Copenhagen summit-meeting and, from that moment on, the meetings followed one another with almost indecent haste. In June 1974, the Bonn Conference outlining the programme. In July, the

Paris Conference where they founded the «Parliamentary Association for Euro-Arab Cooperation». In September, the Damascus Conference. In October, the Rabat one...

*   *   *

I write these dates and, while I do, I feel a kind of disbelief. Because it was not a conspiracy plotted in the dark by jailbirds known only to Police Headquarters: it was an event enacted in the light of day, in front of the television cameras and led by famous leaders, well-known politicians. People to whom citizens had given their votes, their trust. In other words, a conspiracy which could have been prevented. Or opposed, neutralized. The fact is that those bastards acted precisely by exploiting the light of day. The cameras, the spotlights, their prestige or alleged prestige. With such brazenness, such shamelessness, that nobody realized what they were doing. Nobody suspected the betrayal they were committing against their own countries. Against their own civilization. And we, their victims, got fooled like the Prefect of Paris in the story by Edgar Allan Poe.

Do you know that story by Edgar Allan Poe, *The Purloined Letter*? Here it is. A man of genius and devoid of any moral principles, a monstrum-horrendum capable of any iniquity, the famous Minister D, steals a highly important letter from the royal boudoir. A document, a treasure, that can bring incalculable benefits to him and incalculable ruin to the world. The Prefect of Paris must therefore retrieve it and since he is unable to accuse such an important figure of theft, he organizes a fake robbery. He gets into his house or better his palace and searches every hall, every room, every corridor, every wardrobe, every nook and cranny. He rummages in every drawer, leafs through every book, searches every garment. But in vain. Because, instead of hiding his treasure, the monstrum-horrendum has left it in full view. He has put it in a card-rack tied to a blue silk ribbon hanging from the fireplace in his study. The room where he receives all visitors, the fireplace that everybody looks when entering the room. And a card-rack from which the letter protrudes by an inch with its seal. By the way, the seal belonging to the important person. Recognizable, visible even for a blind. Yet the Prefect of Paris does not see it. Better: he sees it but the idea that it might be in full view, at anybody's mercy, does not even occur to him.

I mean: we saw them well at those meetings, those conferences and assemblies. The heads of State, the ministers, the ambassadors, all of them drinking orange juice with the sheikhs and the emirs and the colonels and the sultans. We saw them on the TV news, we saw them on the newspapers: as visible as a card-rack tied up to a blue silk ribbon. But we didn't suspect that the purloined letter was in their orange-juice glasses. And this made us blind. At the Damascus Conference, the European governments took part (would you believe it) with the representatives of all political parties. Right and Left. At the Rabat Conference, they reiterated their deal over the conditions posed by the Arab League in regard to Israel. In Strasbourg the Parliamentary Association for Euro-Arab Cooperation even established a Standing Committee of no fewer than three hundred and sixty officials to be based in Paris. (A measure followed by the Cairo Convention and then by the Rome Convention). And it was then that the little journal with the terrifying name of *Eurabia* came to light. It was then that Europe definitely sold itself to Islam. The fact appears so obvious, and so disquieting, that to verify it I went to Paris and got hold of the back numbers of *Eurabia*. (Printed in Paris. Written in French. Edited by Mr. Lucien Bitterlin. Format 21 by 28. Price five francs). In the hope that Bat Ye'or had misunderstood something I checked all and alas: she had understood very well. In the first issue in fact the only ambiguity is the extreme care with which each article avoids the words Islam, Islamic, Muslim, Koran, Mohammed, Allah. In their place, the words Arabs and Arabia. All the rest is such a confirmation of the sinister plot that Mr. Bitterlin underlines how the future of Europe is directly linked to the future of Middle East and says that any economic agreement has to depend on political agreements: to reflect a «complete identity of European views with the views of the Arab world». In the second issue he goes even further. Because, with a peevish editorial, he demands the European Economic Community to cancel any agreement with Israel and to claim the «millennial contribution made by the Arabs to universal civilization». Then he enumerates the proposals offered by the Strasbourg Resolution, and do you know what the Strasbourg Resolution was about? Future immigrants. To be precise, the immigrants that Arab countries intend to send to Europe along with the oil.

Listen to this, listen: «A medium and long term policy must be formulated through the technology that from now on the European Community will provide the Arab countries in exchange of crude oil and Arab manpower reserves. (Manpower meaning immigrants). With the inclusion of manpower reserves such exchange will lead to the recycling of petro-dollars and to the complete economic integration between Europe and Arabia». And later: «The Parliamentary Association for Euro-Arab Cooperation calls on European governments to prepare special measures to safeguard the free movement of Arab workers who will immigrate to Europe, as well as respect for their fundamental rights. These rights must be and will be equivalent to those of national citizens. Furthermore they will have to establish equal treatment in employment, housing, health care, free schooling, etcetera». Nor does it end here. Because, always carefully avoiding the words Islam, Islamic, Muslim, Koran, Mohammed, Allah, the Strasbourg Resolution goes on talking about the needs that will arise when the «human trade goods» will get to Europe. First of all, «the need to enable immigrants and their families to observe the religious and cultural life of the Arabs». Then, «the necessity to use the press and the various information outlets to create a climate favourable to the immigrants and to their families». Finally, «the urgency to exalt through the press and the academic world the immense contribution given by Arab culture to European development». A theme, this one, retaken at the Cairo Convention by the Committee of Experts

in the following way: «Together with the inalie-
nable right to practise their religion and habits
plus maintain close links with their countries of
origin, the immigrants shall have the right to ex-
port their culture to Europe. That is, to propagate and disseminate Islamic religion and habits».
Understand?!?

At the Cairo Convention, the Committee of
Experts did something else. It clarified that from
the purely technological field the European cooperation had to expand into banking, financial,
scientific, nuclear, industrial, and commercial
fields. Worse: it stated that in addition to sending
«manpower» the Arab countries would purchase
from Europe «massive quantities of weapons».
Something which does not surprise. Wasn't it in
the late Seventies that France began to build the
nuclear complex in Iraq? Wasn't it in the late Seventies that our cities began to fill with «manpower», that is with the car-windows washers who
tormented the car-drivers or the street-sellers who
sold pencils and chewingum? In 1978, I remember it well, they were already occupying the Historical Center of Florence. «But when did they get
here?!?» I asked the tobacconist of piazza Repubblica where they assembled with particular delight. He spread his arms and sighed: «God
knows. One morning I woke up and here they we-

re. Might it be that they parachuted during the night by order of the sheikhs who charge us a billion liras for a drop of gasoline?». Not only: wasn't it in the late Seventies that Arabs started coming to Europe for their shopping? Wasn't it then that Gaddafi bought 10 percent of FIAT? Wasn't it then that the Egyptian Al Fayed started eyeing Harrods of London? They bought up everything. Everything! Shoeshops, big hotels, steel works, old castles, airlines, publishing and film companies, old shops in via Tornabuoni and Faubourg-Saint-Honoré, astronomically-priced yachts... At one point, they even wanted to buy the water. I was told it by Yamani.

* * *

In August 1975, that is two months after the Strasbourg Resolution and the Cairo Convention, I interviewed Saudi oil minister Zaki Yamani: the sheikh who had led the 1973 embargo and who more than anybody else financed Arafat's inexhaustible craving for money. There are many things about Yamani that I shall never forget. First of all the highly astute examination which in no fewer than five preliminary meetings (London, Jeddah, Ryadh, Damascus, Beirut) he put me through before granting the interview that finally took place in his residence at Taif. Then the acumen with which at Jeddah airport he prevented a further clash between me and Arafat who happened to be there. Then the distress with which he told me of the beheading (with a gold sword) of the young prince who had assassinated king Faisal, and the obsequiousness with which he sought my compliance by stuffing my mouth with the awful figs of his garden. The lamb's eye (a most supreme delicacy, apparently) that one day he tried to put in my mouth like the figs. How revolting. And the elegance with which, Koran notwithstanding, he offered me the champagne in which his Taif cellar abounded of. And the charm with which more than once he proposed to accompany me to Mecca, see the Black Stone and thus obtain the blessing of Allah. «But non-Muslims cannot go to Mecca: it's forbidden!» I objected. «You will wear a chador and nobody will know that you are not a Muslim» he answered. «But I have blue eyes and Arab women do not have blue eyes» I insisted. «Arab women have blue eyes as frequently as Western ones» he argued. «But your wife wouldn't like you to escort me to Mecca. Will she come too?» I emphasized. «She will not, and she will not protest. Arab wives are obedient» was the answer. He really didn't want to give up the damn trip to Mecca where, in the end, I did not go. I did not want to go... Nor shall I ever forget the melancholy song his daughter Maha used to sing when she played the guitar: «Oh, take me away! Please, take me away!». But the most unforgettable thing remains what he told me when the conversation wandered from oil and touched upon water. Upon King Midas who is dying of thirst and longs to buy water.

«Thousands and thousands of years ago» he said «in Arabia we had rivers and lakes. Then they evaporated and today we haven't got a single river, a single lake. Go on a helicopter tour and all you'll see is a few exiguous streams. Believe me: since Mohammed's times here in Saudi Arabia we have depended on rain alone. And during the last hundred years very little rain has fallen, indeed. In the last twenty-five, virtually none. Clouds are drawn by vegetation, we know. Desert has no vegetation. Underground the desert some water exists, true. But very, very deep down. Deeper down than oil. And when we drill for it, we find oil... So we content ourselves with desalinated water obtained from seawater. But desalinated water is not enough, and I would like to buy real water from the countries to which we sell oil. Buy it, put it in big plastic containers, and transfer it to reservoirs. I mean into artificial lakes. After unloading

the oil, tankers have to come back: don't they?
And they certainly cannot come back empty. Sailing empty they risk to capsize. So, not to have
them sailing empty and capsize, we fill them with
seawater. Dirty water. And this is a waste. It's also
a mistake because when tankers come back we
flush them out and dirty water pollutes our coasts,
kills our fish. All right: real water, fresh water, is
expensive. And artificial lakes even more. They
cost an enormity. But money is the only stuff we
don't lack. We have even too much of it. We have
so much of it since the embargo, we have accumu-
lated so much of it, that now we're faced with the
urgent problem of spending it. And where should
we spend it if not in the West, in Europe? Who else could help us to invest all that richness if not
the West, not Europe? America is too far away. As
a consequence I have made a plan to spend in Europe 140 billion dollars for five years. If this plan
is not put into effect, we are ruined. So it is worth-
while for us to buy your water and sooner or later
you'll sell it us».

Well... We didn't sell to him, to them, that
kind of water. The water to be put in the reservoirs,
I mean. The water which is defined by dictionaries
as a «transparent, colourless, odourless, tasteless li-
quid composed of oxygen and hydrogen, essential
for vegetable and animal life, known in chemistry

with the formula H$_2$O». However, we did sell them an equally precious water. A water which is as essential to Life as the water of the rivers, as the springs. A water without which people perish like trees on which the rain doesn't fall so they wither, don't blossom any longer, no longer give fruits, and lose their leaves then their branches then their roots and become firewood. I speak of the water which is the water of our culture. The water of our principles, of our values, of our achievements. The water of our language, of our religion, of our secularism, of our History. The water of our essence, of our civilization. The water of our identity.

CHAPTER 7

Yes, we did sell that water to him. We did sell that water to them. Then and after. Since at least thirty years we sell it to them every day. More and more, with the sinister voluptuousness of the servants and of the suicides. We sell it through our fearful and incapable governments. We sell it through our parliamentary oppositions, through the double-crossers and the turncoats who betray their secular and revolutionary past. We sell it through our so-called judicial authorities, that is, through our conceited and publicity-thirsty judges. We sell it through the newspapers and the TV channels which for profit or cowardice preach Political Correctness. We sell it through a Catholic Church which in the name of ecumenism has built on the invaders the industry of pity. Because it is the Catholic associations which administrate State benefits to immigrants. It is the Catholic associations which oppose their expulsions even when they are caught with explosives or drugs. It is the Catholic associations which grant them political asylum: the new tool of the invasion. (By the way:

didn't political asylum use to be given to people who are politically persecuted in or by their country? By whom are these hordes of immigrants politically persecuted?). We also sell it through the little professors of the universities. The historians or alleged historians, the philosophers or alleged philosophers, the scholars or alleged scholars who for thirty years have been denigrating our culture and trying to prove the Superiority-of-Islam. But, above all, we sell it through the merchants of the Financial Club that yesterday we called European Economic Community and today we call European Union. Because, along with the trading of human goods and oil, (send-me-the-oil-and-I'll-take-the-human-goods), the Strasbourg Resolution put forward another demand. Remember? The need to «exalt the immense contribution given by Arab culture to the European development». Along with the warning «immigrants' rights equal to the rights of citizens», the Cairo Convention established the «immigrants' right to propagate and disseminate the Islamic culture». Remember? The two points which drove to the transformation of Europe into Eurabia.

Under the patronage of the Arab League's Secretary General, on March 28th 1977 the Ca' Foscari University in Venice opened the first «Seminar on the Means and Forms of Cooperation for the Dissemination of the Arabic Language and its Literary Civilization». A masochism to which also the Vatican Institute of Arab and Islamic Studies participated. With delegates from ten Arab countries (Egypt, Algeria, Tunisia, Libya, Saudi Arabia, Jordan, Syria, Iraq, Yemen and Sudan) and eight European countries (Italy, France, Belgium, Holland, Britain, Germany, Denmark, Greece) the sad affair lasted three days, and concluded with an unanimous Resolution which called for «the diffusion of the Arabic language» as well as for «the *superiority* of Arab culture». And, from then on, the masochism became boundless. All over Europe it was as if the so called Academic World had lost any control, any common sense. The world of journalism, publishing, film-making, the same: whoever defined himself or herself as an "intellectual" seemed to live in the obsession of demonstrating *la grandeur* of Islam, the *superiority* of Islam. And everything served the purpose. Falsehood, deceit, mendacity. More or less, what happens in Zamiatin *We* and in Orwell *1984*: the novels where history get rewritten, reinvented, without any decency. Take what happened in April 1983 when German Foreign Minister Hans-Dietrich Genscher opened the Hamburg Symposium for the Euro-Arab Dialogue and for an hour he extolled the greatness, the mercy, the benignity, the peerless scientific and humanistic rich-ness of Islamic civilization. He called it a «Beacon of Light, a light that for centuries had illuminated Europe, helped Europe escape its barbarism»... That symposium where almost everybody apolo-gized for the iniquities (Crusades, colonialism, et-cetera) that ungrateful Europeans had inflicted on the Beacon of Light. Where everybody expres-sed contempt for those who still nourished doubts or prejudices about Islam. Where our culture was so belittled that the Arab delegates exploited the opportunity for claiming once more the Islamic origins of Judaism and Christianity, for presenting Abraham as a «prophet of Allah» and Jesus Christ as a failed pre-Mohammed. And nobody who da-red to protest, to oppose at least an indignant: Ha-ve you lost your mind?!?

Oh! They spoke of immigrants too, in that symposium. Sure they did. In fact it was there that the term used by the Arab League for the immi-grants, «equivalence», became «equality». It was there that our traitors began to say that the rights of Muslim immigrants (not Buddhist or Hindu or Confucian or Greek Orthodox) must be equal to the rights of the host countries' citizens. It was the-re that they asked us to print newspapers in Arabic, to open radio stations and television channels broadcasting in Arabic. It was there that they requested to «increase their presence in trade-unions, in local administrations, in universities, and asked to explore the prospect of their participation in the political life of the host countries». (Read vote). And, from that day on, all the conferences and meetings and seminars and symposiums became more and more an orgiastic apotheosis of Islamic-civilization. A debasement or a condemnation of western civilization.

Absolutely orgiastic. I have collected many complete proceedings of those conferences and meetings and seminars and symposiums, I have studied them, and for God's sake! In each one the apotheosis is so unanimous that it seems to read *Allahs Sonne über dem Abendland*. That is *The Sun of Allah Shines over the West*: the famous essay in which oriental studies scholar Sigrid Hunke argues the absolute superiority of Islam and states that «the influence exerted by the Arabs on the West was the first step in freeing Europe from Christianity». The trouble is that Mrs. Hunke was a fucking Nazi. As learned as you like, as intelligent as you want, but a fucking Nazi. She was already such in 1935 when at the age of twenty-two she produced a degree thesis claiming that racial purification was an urgent task. Thus, the Jews had to be eliminated in a hurry. She was even more such in 1937 when, the spiritual heiress of Ludwig Ferdinand Clauss (an eminent historian of National-Socialist Germany), she wrote a dissertation where she called Hitler «the best model that History has ever offered to Germany». She was such and more than ever in the early Forties, when together with her sister she joined the Germanistischer Wissenschafteinsatz: the German Sciences Service of the SS, the organization conceived and run by Himmler to oversee the Germanization of northern Europe. She was just as much when in the same years the Palestinians and the other Arabs signed alliances with Hitler. For example when the Grand Mufti of Jerusalem and uncle of Arafat reviewed the troops of the Islamic SS. (Have you ever seen the photo?). The same, at the aftermath of the Second World War, when many Nazis were tried at Nuremburg and hanged but she got off unscathed. The same, when in 1960 she wrote her famous book. A book which with the pretext of tearing Europe off its Judaic-Christian roots proposes again the axioms of the Third Reich. Including the alliance with the Arabs in order to fight British imperialism. (In those days anti-Americanism was called anti-Britishism). The same, in 1967 when the German government led by Christian Democrat Kurt Georg Kiesinger sent her on a cultural tour of Arab countries to give lectures in Aleppo, Algiers, Tunis, Tripoli, Cairo where the Supreme Court of Islamic Affairs appointed her an honorary member. And, more than ever, she was such in 1990. That is when, nine years before dying, she wrote for an Islamic publisher her last book: *Allah ist ganz anders*: *Allah is something else entirely*. (Meaning, something unparalleled. Matchless, incomparable). This said, let me tell you about the conference which along with the Council of Europe and at the suggestion of the Fundación Occidental de la Cultura Islámica, longa manus of the Euro-Arab Dialogue in Madrid, the Parliamentary Assembly of the European Union held in May 1991 in Paris. Title, «The contribution of Islamic civilization to European culture». A conference which the Arabs did not even care to attend. Apart from two Americans with Koranesque surnames, this time all the delegates were European. I mean Spanish, French, Belgian, German, Italian, Swiss, Scandinavian.

Among all the material I have assembled in the last years, I choose it because they were all Europeans. And, as I read again the volume containing their speeches, my indignation turns into dismay. In fact all the participants who take part in the apotheosis echo Sigrid Hunke's Nazi propositions. Unawarely, I hope, they rephrase to *Allahs Sonne über dem Abendland* or *Allah ist ganz anders*. And the synchronization with which these

159

hopefully-unaware disciples of Sigrid Hunke pay their homage to Islam is chilling. So chilling that instead of listening to a conclave of scholars, you feel like watching a Wehrmacht parade in Alexanderplatz. Always clever, the Muslims. Always at the top. Always ingenious. In philosophy, in mathematics, in gastronomy, in literature, in architecture, in medicine, in music, in law, in hydraulics, in cooking. And always stupid, we westerners. Always inadequate, always inferior. Therefore obliged to thank some son of Allah who preceded us. Who enlightened us. Who acted as a schoolteacher guiding dimwitted pupils.

* * *

In the days of the Soviet Union there was Popov. Nobody knew who Popov was or had been. When or in what region he had lived or died, what his face had been like, what proof of his existence he had left. It was not even known whether the name Popov was a first name or a surname or a nickname or an invention. But the Soviets and the Italian servants of the Soviets used to tell us that he had invented everything. The train, the telegraph, the telephone, the bicycle, the zipper, the sewing machine, the lawnmower, the violin, the ice-cream, the pizza. I mean all the things that we thought the West had invented. Well: with the hopefully-unaware-disciples of Sigrid Hunke, it's quite the same. Only difference, their Popovs are called Muhammad or Ahmad or Mustafa or Rashid. And instead of belonging to the Soviet Union, instead of representing the superiority of Communism, they belong to the past of Islam and represent the superiority of Islam. For example: I believed that the sherbet was already eaten at the time of the Ancient Romans who manufactured it with snow brought from the mountains and conserved it in cold cellars. But Margarita López Gómez of the «Fundación Occidental de la Cultura Islámica in Madrid» tells me that it was invented by the Popovs of Allah. That in Mesopotamia the snow could be conserved better than in our modern refrigerators. That the word «sherbet» comes from the Arabic «sharab».

I also believed that paper had been invented by the Chinese. To be precise, by a certain Tsai-lun who in 105 Anno Domini (therefore 500 years before the Prophet) succeeded in manufacturing paper from mulberry and bamboo fibres. But, always according to Margarita López Gómez, paper was invented by the Muslims of Damascus and Baghdad then widespread by their descendants in Cordoba and in Granada. (The «most splendid and civilized cities the world had ever known», she says. The two marvels which made Pericles' Athens and Augustus' Rome look like squalid villages, she would like us to think). I also believed that the study of blood circulation had been initiated by Hippocrates. But according to Mrs. López Gómez it was initiated by Ibn Sina that is to say Avicenna, without whom Medicine would not have survived. Nor does it end here. Because, according to Professor Sherif Mardin of Washington University, (one of the two Americans with a Koranesque surname), to the Popovs of Islam we owe even the artichokes. Including the *carciofi alla giudea*, the fried artichokes that in Italy we attribute to the Jews. And, along with the *carciofi alla giudea*, we owe Islam an incredible amount of fruits and vegetables and cereals. Spinach, oranges, lemons, sorgum, beans, cotton. (Funny, this cotton thing, given the fact that cotton was imported by the ancient Romans from the Egyptians at the time of the pharaohs, meaning long before the birth of the Prophet. That Egyptians used cotton to make pepluses, togas, sheets. And, if I'm not mistaken, the ancient Greeks did the same. Again, long before the birth of the Prophet).

Professor Mardin, however, does not stop at vegetables. At cereals, at cotton, at paper and ice-cream. He maintains that to Islamic civilization we also owe the Dolce Stil Novo: the poetic school which, as everybody knows, was founded in the 13th century by the Bolognese Guinizelli but flourished in Tuscany. Especially in Florence with Dante Alighieri and Guido Cavalcanti and Lapo Gianni. («Guido, I wish that Lapo and you and I...» begins the Dante's sonnet we studied at school). Because it was the Muslims of the Crusades the first ones to sing of love and courtliness and chivalry, professor Mardin explains. It was their civilization that saw the Woman as a fount of inspiration, a mystic instrument of edification. Professor Louis Baeck of the Catholic University of Louvain in Belgium, ditto or worse. In fact he states that the contribution of Islam is not confined to literature: it extends to economics. The father of economic theory, he says, is not Adam Smith: it is the Prophet himself. Although the Koran devotes to economics a few Surahs only, the religious norms that the Prophet expresses through them subsume all Adam Smith's ideas. Professor Reinhard Schulze of the Orientalist Seminar in Bonn, instead, ascribes to Islam the full paternity of Enlightenment. Enough, he roars, with attributing the Enlightenment to the West. Enough with presenting Europe of the Eighteenth Century as a volcano of intellectual vitality. Islam, as an abyss of inertia and decadence. Enough with assigning every merit to the Voltaires, the Rousseaus, the Diderots, the Encyclopaedists. Then he delightedly reveals to us his Enlightenment's Popov. He is Abdalghani Al-Nabulusi, a historian from Damascus who as early as in 1730 wrote what Voltaire was to write forty-three years later in his *Précis sur le Procès du Monsieur le Comte de Morangies contre la Famille Verron*. That is, the necessity of redefining the role of religion in society.

(Letter to professor Schulze: «Dear Sir, shut up your big mouth and leave certain theories to your compatriot Sigrid Hunke. We know perfectly well that in Islam's historic past there have been a few intelligent, exceptional men. Intelligence doesn't know borders, it always manages to penetrate the wall of constitutionalized idiocy, so in 1730 your Popov from Damascus might have shared or even anticipated some of the Encyclopaedists' ideas. For example, through reading Isaac Newton who on that subject had already published a treatise on history and one on theology. But, aside from the fact that a single swallow doesn't bring the summer, Islam has always persecuted and silenced its intelligent men. I remind you of Averroës who for his distinction between Faith and Reason was accused of heterodoxy by the caliphs and forced to flee. Then, imprisoned like a criminal. Then, confined to his home and humiliated to such a degree that when rehabilitated he no longer had any desire to live and died within a few months. Not without good reason, in his famous lecture held in 1883 at the Sorbonne, Ernest Renan said that attributing the merits of Averroës to Islam would be like attributing the merits of Galileo to the Inquisition. Herr Schulze! If there is a century in which Islam radiated nothing but inertia and decadence, this is just the Eighteenth. And if there is a current of thought with which Islam has never had a damn thing to do, this is just the Enlightenment. You know why? Because, as Diderot wrote two hundred and forty-five years ago to Madame Volland: "Islam is the enemy of Reason". And if your Muslim friends don't open a little your brains, if your brains don't give the Koran and theocracy a good rinsing, no Eurabia will ever be able to prove the opposite». End of the letter).

As for the Italians who at that conference distinguished themselves for their homage to Islam... Oh, Jesus! One was the Vice-Secretary General of the Council of Europe: an ex-Socialist. One was an ex-Communist who headed the Commission for Youth and Culture and Sport and Media of the European Parliament. One occupied the chair in Islamic Studies at the pro-Islamic University of Naples. And reading their speeches imbues me with consternation. Blinded by the Beacon-of-Light, in fact, the first one finds Popov even in traditional Neapolitan songs. In "'O sole mio", for instance, and "Funiculì-Funiculà". «The Neapolitan songs I sing may well have been written by a musician of North Africa» he asserts, «and the same may be said of a great number of Sicilian or Spanish songs». (I read the text I have in front of my eyes). Then from musical homage he too moves on to gastronomic homage. He informs us that many Sicilian, Spanish, Bulgarian, Greek and Yugoslav dishes (that is the countries most mangled by Islamic colonialism) belong to the culinary art of the Moors or of the Ottoman Empire. From gastronomic homage he moves to theological homage and, forgetting or not knowing a celebrated work called *De unitate intellectus contra Averroistas*, informs us that St. Thomas Aquinas was profoundly influenced by the Averroës School. On the other hand, the second Italian runs down Giambattista Vico. He declares that his theory of History cyclical pattern had already been formulated three hundred years earlier by a Popov called Ibn Khaldun. And, not satisfied with that, he devalues Marco Polo. He boasts that the *Chronicles* of the traveller Ibn Battuta are far more interesting than Marco Polo's *Travels*. He also cuts down Giordano Bruno. He

166

upbraids us for shedding tears over his burning alive and for not doing the same over the same martyrdom of the Muslim Al-Hallaj. Finally, he defines Islam as «one of the most extraordinary political and moral forces in the world of today». (Not of yesterday: of today). He reveals that, far from having an identity of its own, European culture is a mixture of cultures among which Islamic culture must be included as the first. He also welcomes «the integration which is *ennobling our continent*» and hopes that multi-culturalism will reinvigorate us more and more...

The third Italian does almost worse: he extends the glories of Andalusia to Sicily subjugated for three centuries by the real composers of "'O sole mio" and "Funiculì-Funiculà". Ignoring the fact that for almost a century the Sicilians fought against the Muslim invaders like lions, in that Sicily he sees another Golden Age. An age so glorious, so happy, that you conclude: being invaded again by the sons of Allah is the biggest piece of luck we could have. Rather than complaining we should be thanking them on our knees. «Shukran, brothers, shukran! We are grateful for your coming and bringing civilization again!». He even reveals that in the Golden Age Sicily many Christians asked to be converted to Islam. And not at the purpose of acquiring the rights denied to infidel-dogs but because they profoundly admired those Popovs. He also adds that the Normans, their chasers, admired them as much. And it goes without saying that during the Conference Belgian and French delegates outdo him a lot. In his passionate encomium, for instance, the Director of the Paris Institut du Monde Arabe, Professor Edgar Pisani, reproach the Jacobins who during the French Revolution negotiated with the Catholic Church and not with Islam.

* * *

Look, in these one hundred and eighty-five pages I can see only one hero: the Norwegian congressman Hallgrim Berg who at the Strasbourg Assembly convened to approve the conference report, took the floor and gave Sigrid Hunke's disciples a good answer. «Ladies and gentlemen» he said «here we are fooling ourselves: this report has nothing to do with a retrospective view of Islamic Culture and is not as innocent as it looks. It is not, first of all, because it does not spend a word for the abominable treatment that women undergo and have always undergone in the Islamic culture. Such indisputable fact has been completely ignored by you, completely covered up under the pretext that Westerners have always told a pack of lies about Islam. And I shall never accept a report which hides the tragedy of Muslim women instead of taking a stand against it. I shall never vote for a report which avoids the question of Human Rights in Islam. Which blathers of Human Rights in the world but does not ask Islam to respect Human Rights in its world. A report, furthermore, which hides the truth about the Israeli-Palestinian problem. Which covers up the crimes of Islamic fundamentalism and all the other negative features of Islam. Ladies and gentlemen, which kind of Euro-Arab Dialogue are you chattering about?!? Yours is no dialogue. It's a solitary diatribe where, in the name of liberal thought and of intellectual generosity, things are seen from one point of view only. But liberal thought and intellectual generosity don't work when they exist on one side only. You ask, for instance, for the withdrawal of school texts which make no mention of the presumed «contribution made by Islam to the culture of Europe». But what about the contribution that the West has given and gives to their progress? Have we any evidence of their intention to explain in Islamic countries the immense contribution that Christianity and Western values have brought everywhere? You also ask to introduce the study of

Koranic Law in our educational system. Especially in our universities. What about the introduction of our Law in their educational system, their universities? Have we any reason to believe that such study will ever be permitted in their schools? Ladies and gentlemen, your report is not a cultural document. It is a political document which serves exclusively the purpose of underpinning the Islamic interests all over Europe. In the name of democracy I ask that it be revised, discussed, rectified, and...». But it was no use. «Mr. Berg, you must admit that we have been very flexible with you. We've allowed you five minutes, and the five minutes have passed a long time ago» interrupted the president of the Assembly. Then he put Berg's request to the vote, Berg's request was rejected, and the report was approved unanimously. It became «Recommandation Numéro 1162 sur la Contribution de la Civilization Islamique à la Culture Européenne». A piece of tomfoolery that suggests more tolerant rules on immigration and calls for the withdrawal of Western school texts not sufficiently respectful to Islam. It also calls for the introduction of Koran studies in our faculties of law, theology, philosophy and history.

Not surprisingly, I came to learn that soon after the approval of the Recommandation Numéro 1162 Mr. Berg abandoned politics. He left Strasbourg Parliament, went back to Norway, and threatening to throw off the cliffs anyone who reminded him of the European Parliament he retired to a forest overlooking the fjords of Nordkinnhalvaya. But not even there did he find the peace he longed for. Because a couple of years later his Norway was used as the setting for a film entitled «The Thirteenth Knight»: a sort of medieval fable interpreted by a Spanish actor who had previously distinguished himself playing Mussolini as a young socialist: Antonio Banderas. And do you know who is, the «Thirteenth Knight»? A most handsome, most mild, most merciful and of course most religious Muslim who, escorted by a no less perfect tutor (Omar Sharif) in the Tenth Century ends up right among the fjords of Nordkinnhalvaya. There he meets twelve obtuse and ignorant blond louts who, being infidel-dogs, are in need of his Islamic virtues. Out of pure nobility he joins them, together with them he establishes peace and civilization. Then he reunites with Omar Sharif who being a Muslim and therefore a pacifist had stayed behind to pray and, carrying off a Norwegian girl clearly destined to become the first of four wives, rides off into the sun. The Sun-of-Allah-that-shines-over-the-West.

Well, I never found out if Mr. Berg ever recovered or not from the trauma. In return I know that in subsequent European Union's conferences The Recommandation Numéro 1162 was extended to philology, linguistics, economics, agronomy, political science. That it exhorted to establish Euro-Arab universities in every country of Europe, to publish more Islamic books, to mobilize all the media. And the results were immediate. Last summer a leftist Rome newspaper, *La Repubblica*, printed an article on the opening of the great mosque in Granada. More than an article, a Sigrid Hunke hymn to the glory of the Prophet. Recalling that in 1492 Isabella of Castile had not only completed the expulsion of the Moors from Spain but had also financed the voyage of Christopher Columbus to the West Indies, the hymn concluded with the following words: «Columbus succeeded. But he also discovered America. And now we live in a world which is still suffering from the success of those Isabella's two enterprises».

CHAPTER 8

I must not forget those words that seem to have gushed out from Sigrid Hunke's brain. I must not because on 12 of November 2003, in Nassiriyah, the knights of the «Sun-of-Allah-that-shines-over-the-West» massacred nineteen Italian soldiers who were in Iraq acting as guardian angels. Who provided the Iraqi population with water and food and medicines. Who guarded the archeological sites and recovered treasures stolen from museums. Who confiscated weapons and tried to restore some public order. The knights of the Sun of Allah massacred them as three days earlier they had massacred seventeen Saudis in Riyadh and before that twenty-four UN officials in Baghdad, and before that forty-five civilians in Casablanca and before that thirty-four in Riyadh. As in 2002 they had massacred the two hundred and two tourists in Bali and the twenty-one in Djerba. As in 2001 they had massacred the three thousand five hundred in New York and Washington and Pennsylvania. As in 1998 they had massacred the two hundred and fifty-nine in Nairobi and Dar es-

Salaam. As in 1994 they had massacred the ninety-five (almost all Jews) in Buenos Aires and in 1993 the eighteen Marines of a peacekeeping mission at Mogadishu. (The eighteen whose bodies were mutilated, torn in pieces, and dragged along the streets of the city while the mob happily yelled «Allah akbar, Allah akbar!»). And in 1992 the twenty-nine tourists of Buenos Aires, in 1989 the one hundred and seventy-one passengers of the French airliner which went down in the Niger desert. And in 1988, the two hundred and seventy passengers of the Pan American aircraft blown up over the Scottish town of Lockerbie. in 1983 the two hundred and forty-one American soldiers and the fifty-eight French soldiers (also on a peacekeeping mission) in Beirut. This not counting the Israelis who for half a century have been slaughtered on a monotonous daily basis. Only since the Second Intifada, end of September 2000, a thousand Israelis. Which, excluding the victims of the Seventies, means a total of over six thousand dead in more than twenty years. Six thousand! Dead for the glory of the Koran. In obedience to its Surahs. For example the Surah that says: «The reward for those who corrupt the Earth opposing Allah and his Prophet is to be hung or decapitated or crucified. Or to have their hands and feet amputated and be banished with contempt from this world». Yet the

174

Sigrid-Hunke's disciples for whom the year 1492 was a calamity, the discovery of America and the chasing of the Moors from Spain two catastro-phies-from-which-mankind-has-never-recovered, refuse to admit it.

Take the case of Italy. That November 12 the TV-News opened, yes, with the President of the Republic carrying out his duty of condemning terrorism. It continued, yes, with emphasizing that obvious condemnation. It even bestowed us with the unusual image of a Parliament that ex-pressed by not degenerating in the usual uproars. But it concluded with the Secretary of the Italian Communists Party, (minister of Justice at the time of the Center-Left government), who instead of blaming the massacre's authors blamed the go-vernment. «It-was-the-government-that-sent-our-boys-to-their-death». Ergo, that night the Italians went to sleep with those words in their ears. Not with disdain for the real culprits. The next day, ditto. Because the next day he repeated that in any way the slaughter's responsibility had to be attri-buted to the government. Then, giving the im-pression that the fall of Saddam Hussein was ano-ther calamity for mankind, he said that in Iraq the Italians had joined an «imperial and colonial war». Still worse: using the language of the doc-tors at Pinocchio's deathbed, if-he's-not-dead-

he's-alive-and-if-he's-not-alive-he's-dead, the whole
Left demanded the withdrawal of our troops in
Iraq. (Since then, their favourite refrain). And
among leftist congressmen the term «Resistance»
began to spread. As for the so-called Exponents
of the Islamic Communities, that is the Drafts of
Agreement's authors, not one expressed a word of
condemnation or even regret. Not one. All of them
presented the massacre as the result of a legitimate «people's resistance». And the Union of Islamic
Communities declared that the nineteen victims
of Nassiriyah had been sent to Iraq in «contempt
of the fundamental values of the Italian Republic». The imam of the biggest mosque in Naples
said that «the West was causing more deaths than
the two World Wars put together», and consequently the Muslim Nation had to defend itself.
«If the West does not change direction, it will be
struck by our Muslim brothers». The imam of the
Ascoli Piceno's mosque, instead, said that «the attacks on the Anglo-American-Italian invaders of
Iraq and Afghanistan were and are part of a most
legitimate Jihad and obeyed yet obey the Koran's
teaching». The imam of the Islamic Cultural Center in Bologna said that «the kamikazes blown up
in Nassiriyah had died for a just cause: thus the
Prophet would reward them and Allah would fill
them with glory».

As for the Combonian Fathers, the friars who waving rainbow scarves go around distributing Residence-Permits-in-the-name-of-God, they proclaimed that administering the Holy Communion to soldiers in Iraq was wrong. «If we deny such sacrament to those who divorce and practise abortion, how can we administer it to those who carry weapons and with weapons are ready to kill?». Finally, on November 16, during Sunday Mass in the cathedral, the Bishop of Caserta pronounced a homily in which he said that blessing the coffins of the nineteen dead soldiers was like legitimizing the use of arms and woe to whomever would dare to bless them. He also said that it pained to witness the celebrations which took place in their honour.

(Letter to the ungodly Bishop of Caserta. «Dear Bishop, I know that disgracing you in public is a favour that you are not worthy of. In any other circumstance, in fact, I would not accord you a similar satisfaction. But the crime with which you sullied yourself in the cathedral and during the Holy Mass offends not only the nineteen Italians massacred in Nassiriyah: it offends their families, their comrades in arms, the values, the principles, and the honour of our country. It furthermore corrupts the young people, it deceives them, it prevents them from reasoning. It trains a

177

generation of imbeciles. So I hold my nose and I accord you this satisfaction in the hope of not being overcome by the rage that shakes me. Sir, your homily was ignoble. Despicable, indecent, irresponsible. To those nineteen dead you now owe a deep apology. Go to their cemeteries, Sir, and from grave to grave flagellate yourself as the penitents did in the days when sin could not be washed away with two Paternosters and three Ave Marias. Then do the same to apologize with their families and their fellow-soldiers and your Homeland. Though this word, I am sure, means nothing to you. Sir, since you are an individual whose existence until today I was fortunate enough not to be acquainted with, I have conducted a small investigation and found out that you like to exploit your alleged spiritual authority. That despite your venerable age you have a taste for displaying yourself in the role of a radical tough-guy. A role in which you made your debut when, out of boredom for your comfortable life, I guess, you sided with the new Communists. I also found out that you like to show off with little articles, little editorials, little interviews granted to the leftist and extreme leftist papers, and that appealing to the Gospels you always settle on the side of the invaders, for instance claiming that they should vote in our elections. That you call the war in Iraq «an attack to mankind». That you have a lot of respect for Saddam Hussein and Bin Laden. That you unreservedly justify the kamikazes and call their slaughters «acts of Resistence» and even «of heroism». Finally, I have discovered that you speak very badly of the Church that you belong to. The Catholic Church. A right that I can exercise as much as I want and that you cannot. Because I am a free citizen, Sir, and a laic. A person who does not obey anybody and can oppose anybody. On the contrary, you are a party man. A high prelate of the Vatican. A representative of the Pope. To the Catholic Church you owe even the underpants you wear and the shoes you walk in. And as such you cannot run with the hare while hunting with the hounds. You cannot have at the same time the wife drunk and the barrel full of wine. You cannot enjoy the role of Bishop and simultaneously pose as a radical tough-guy. Unless you present your resignations. So, if you wish to speak ill of your benefactors, you must relinquish all: the mitre, the croiser, the cope, the big amethyst ring, the symbols of your authority and also your archiepiscopal palace. Also the bows, the hand-kissing, the obsequiousness of your congregation. And content yourself with being a scribe for the no-globals who burn the cars and sack the McDonald's. Sir, if that Sunday Jesus Christ had had the misfortune to find himself in the Caserta cathedral, his disdain for the Temple's Pharisee merchants would have become a joke in comparison to his disdain for you. He would have kicked your ass and thrown you out into the square and here he would have smashed so hard your face that today you would not even be able to eat a tomato soup». End of the letter). But the discourse continues.

* * *

It does because, twenty-four hours after the non-eminent bishop's exploit, a woman who is defined as «the present head of the Red Brigades», (another misfortune of my country and of the Western civilization), added her voice to the subject of Nassiriyah massacre. She did it at the trial she was standing for the murder of a police officer and by means of a statement that the judge had forbidden her to read during the hearing and that however he had put on record. (So the newspapers would report it all the same). And guess what such dame said. She said that killing the nineteen Italians in peace mission had been a sacrosanct right of the Iraqi kamikazes, pardon, Resistants. That «in order to destroy American imperialism and Zionist entity the Red Brigades had to make a common front with Saddam Hussein and Bin Laden's fighters». That «the Arab masses are the natural allies of the European proletariat», and that the European-proletariat had to join «the heroic Resistance» of Islam. So here is another open letter.

(Letter to the grand dame of the Red Brigades. «Dear young lady. Your presentation of Bin Laden and Saddam Hussein in the guise of Lenin or Mao Tse-tung is as cretinous as insulting for the intelligence of the metropolitan-proletariat. So I wonder how you can be the "brains" of the Red Brigades. If you really are, those brigades don't have a chance. They better look for a job in the mafia, an institution which always need killers. As for the rest, you have no right to use the term Resistance: that is, a term which evokes the fight against Nineteenth Century nazi-fascism. You have no right to compare the Islamic carnages with the battle that our fathers or some of our fathers fought to regain the freedom in which you were born and of which you take advantages like a jackal. Have you any idea of what Resistance meant for our fathers?!? It meant hangings, firing squads, crematory-ovens. It meant interrogations conducted with torture, feet burned, nails ripped out. Cudgels in the mouth, cigarettes extinguished on the breasts and the eyes, electric shocks in the testicles and in the vagina, urine forced down into the throat till suffocation. All things for which you would die of fear at the only hearing of them. It also meant stinking cells where they had to sleep on a filthy floor and defecate in a can brimming with shit. It also meant cockroaches floating in the nauseous muck the guards called soup, rats biting their eyes and wounds. And no journalists to tell about. No Amnesty International to play with. Young lady, it's easy to pose as a warrior in a regime of freedom and democracy. It's easy to preach or give death in a country which does not punish death preachers and givers with the death penalty. It's easy to play the revolutionary when at a trial the judges question courteously and the lawyers defend solicitously and nobody calls you a crap when you vacuously declame: "For-my-political-acts-I-answer-only-to-the-metropolitan-proletariat". It's easy to side with the enemy when the harshest punishment you receive for this betrayal is a cell provided with bed and blankets and sheets and washbasin and water-closet and running water and electricity and books to read and paper to write on. A prison where you choose what to eat as if you were in a restaurant, halal meat if you're a Muslim, and where you can make telephone calls. You can watch television, receive visitors, etcetera. All this, without

considering the amnesties, the penalty-discounts, the lenient and ridiculous permits which get out of prison from morning to evening. As if prisons were kind of hotels free of charge. Yes, it's easy. And convenient and cowardly. Young lady, you are a coward. You are the symbol itself of today's permissive, irresponsible society. The emblem itself of its pusillanimity, of its weakness, its pretentiousness, its superficiality, its stupidity, its lack of knowledge and courage. But courage has never distinguished the types of your type. What kind of audaciousness is required to shoot a policeman who soberly patrols the trucks of a train and who keeping his gun inside the holster politely asks to see your documents? What kind of boldness is required to fill with bullets a defence-less professor who goes home with his bicycle, what kind of guts is required to kill in the same way an unarmed Union-man who walks all alone in a deserted street? Or, given the fact that you are such a good ally of the bastards who want to eliminate me in the name of Allah, what kind of heroism is required to execute a person as fragile as I am, meaning a person whom the lightest gust of wind can knock down? By the way: am I really in the condemned to death list? If so, my dear, go and fuck yourself along with your comrades».
End of the letter).

* * *

Voilà. I have succumbed to temptation. I have allowed myself to be overtaken by the rage which consumes me soon after September 11. But now I feel better, and can talk in detachment about the threesome marriage which has delivered Italy to the enemy. The one I call the Triple Alliance, the ominous pact between the Right and the Left and the Catholic Church. Let's start with the Catholic Church.

CHAPTER 9

I am a Christian atheist. I do not believe in what we imply by the word God. Since the day I realized that I didn't believe in that «what», (something which happened very early in my life, and exactly when I was an adolescent tormented by the grievous dilemma is-there-a-God-or-not), I think that God has been created by men and not vice versa. I think that men have invented Him out of solitude, powerlessness, despair. Meaning, to give an answer to the mystery of existence. To attenuate the insoluble questions that life throws on our faces. Who we are, where do we come from, where we are going. What was here before us and before these worlds, billions and billions of worlds spinning in the universe with such a precision, what will come afterwards... In other words, I think that we invented Him out of weakness, namely out of fear of living and dying. Living is very difficult, dying is always a sorrow, and the concept of a God who helps us to face those two challenges can bring infinite relief: I understand it well. In fact I envy those who believe. At times I am even jealous of them. Never though, never, to the point of developing the suspicion and therefore the hope that a God exists. Or that with all those billions and billions of worlds He has the time to find me, to look after me. Ergo, I get off by myself. As if this weren't enough, I don't stand Churches. Whatever their Credo is. I cannot endure their dogmas, their liturgies, their presumed spiritual authority, their material power. And I don't get along with priests. Even when they are intelligent or innocent, I don't forget that they serve that material power. And there is always a moment when my inborn anti-clericalism re-emerges. A moment when I smile at the ghost of my maternal grandfather who was a 19th-century anarchist and used to sing: «With the guts of priests we shall hang the kings». Nevertheless, I repeat, I am a Christian.

I am even though I reject various Christian precepts. Such as the matter of turning the other cheek, of forgiving. (An error which encourages wickedness and that I never commit). Notwithstanding the refusal of various precepts and particularly forgiveness, clemency, I am a Christian because I like the discourse which stays at the roots of Christianity. Because it convinces me. It seduces me to such an extent that in it I do not find any contradiction with my atheism and my secularism. I mean the discourse conceived by

Jesus of Nazareth, of course, not the one elabora-
ted or distorted or betrayed through the Catholic
and Protestant doctrines. The discourse which tra-
scending metaphysics, climbing over it, concentra-
tes on Man. Which admitting free-will, claiming
Man's conscience, makes us responsible for our
actions. Masters of our destiny. I see a hymn to
Reason, a revival of clear thinking in that discourse. And given the fact that where there is clear
thinking there is choice, where there is choice there is freedom, I see in it the rediscovery of freedom. The redemption of liberty. At the same time
I see in it the surmounting of a God invented by
men out of solitude, out of impotence, of despair,
of weakness and of fear to live and to die. In short,
the dimming of the abstract and omnipotent and
pitiless Gods that almost all religions have shaped
for us. Zeus who incinerates with his lightning
bolts, Jehovah who blackmails with his threats and
his vendettas, Allah who subjugates with his cruel-
ties and senselessnesses. And in the place of those
invisible intangible tyrants an idea that nobody
had ever had. Certainly, never divulged. The idea
of a God that becomes Man. Meaning the idea of
Man who becomes God. God of himself. A God
with two arms and two legs, a God made of flesh
who goes around making or trying to make the Revolution of the Soul. Who speaking of a Creator

seated in Heaven (otherwise who would listen, who would understand?) introduces himself as his Son and explains that all men are brothers of his Son. Therefore equally sons of that God and theoretically capable of exercising their own divine essence. Exercising it by preaching the Goodness which is the fruit of Reason, of Freedom, by spreading Love which before being a feeling is a reasoning. A syllogism or better an enthymeme from which we deduce that goodness is intelligence and wickedness is stupidity.

A God, finally, who faces the problem of Ethics as a man. With the brain of a man, the heart of a man, the words of a man, the deeds of a man. And forget his meekness. Forget his sweetness, his tenderness, his let-the-children-come-unto-me... I often wonder if Jesus of Nazareth temperament really was that meek, that sweet, that tender. And each time I answer myself: maybe not, I guess not. Because as a man, not as a God, he performs the Revolution of the Soul. As a man, not as a God, he takes his fists to the pharisees and to the rabbis who profit by religion. As a man, not as a God, he tackles the theme of secularism that St. Paul will develop. «Render-unto-Caesar-what-belongs-to-Caesar-and-unto-God-what-belongs-to-God». As a man, not as a God, he stops the cowards who are about to stone the adulteress and thunders: «He who is without sin first cast his stone». As a man, not as a God, he blasts against slavery, and let's say it loud and clear: who, before Jesus of Nazareth, had ever blasted against slavery? Who had ever said that slavery, any form of slavery, is unacceptable inadmissible inconceivable? As a man, in conclusion, he fights. He grieves, he suffers, he certainly sins. As a man he dies. Without dying because Life does not die. Life always resurrects, Life is eternal. And, together with the discourse on Reason, on Freedom, this is the point that mostly convinces me. That mostly seduces me. Because in it I see the rejection of Death, the refusal of Death, the apotheosis of Life which can be evil: yes. Which is also evil, which eats itself. But its alternative is Nothingness. And let's face it: such is the principle which leads and feeds our civilization.

* * *

This morning I reread the famous essay that Benedetto Croce published in 1942: *Why we cannot avoid calling ourselves Christians*. (Yes, the one where to the discredit of the idiots who revere Islam as the Beacon-of-Light he observes: «The long age of glory that was called the Middle Ages completed the Christianization of the Barbarians and animated the defence against Islam: the entity which threatens European civilization»). Well, two things in that essay strike me deeply: the incisive judgement with which Croce exalts what I call Revolution of the Soul, and the force with which he argues that all subsequent revolutions have stemmed from it: «Christianity is the greatest revolution humanity has ever accomplished. By comparison, all the others seem limited». Besides we don't need Benedetto Croce to realize that without Christianity there would not have been the Renaissance, there would not have been the Enlightenment, there would not have even been the French Revolution which despite its atrocities originated out of the respect for Man. And which, in that sense, did leave or stimulate positive experiments. To begin with, the socialist experiment which failed so disastrously but, like the French Revolution, did leave or stimulate beneficial results. Still less would there have been Liberalism. That liberalism which we cannot avoid keeping at the base of a civil society, and which today everybody accepts or pretends to accept. In my view, without the Christian Revolution of the Soul, there would not have been either the present waking-up of women. Thus, look: denuded of its parables and fables about miracles and physical resurrections, cleansed of its fundamentalist superstructures, liberated from its doc-

trinaire chains, meaning brought back to the pro-
digious idea of the splendid Nazarene, Christianity
truly is an irresistible provocation. A sensational
bet that Man makes with himself. And here we get
to the faults of a Catholic Church which making
part of the Triple Alliance, favouring Islam, has
borne and bears the prime responsibility for the
catastrophe we are living in.

Because before invading our territory and
destroying our culture, before cancelling our identity, Islam aims to extinguish that irresistible provocation. That sensational bet. You know how? By
its ideological robberies. By its engulfing Christianity, its presenting Christianity in the guise of a de-
generate scion. By its defining Jesus Christ as «a
prophet of Allah». A second-class prophet, of course. So inferior to Mohammed that almost six hundred years later Mohammed had to start again
from scratch. He had to go through his chat with
Archangel Gabriel and, alas, write the Koran. To
better rob us of Jesus, Muslim theologians even
deny that he was crucified: they place him in their
Djanna and make him eat like a Trimalchio, drink
like a drunkard, copulate like a sex-maniac. Then
they utter: «In his own way Jesus preached the
word of Allah, but treacherous disciples distorted
his words and called Christianity what in reality
was already Islam». They also aim to steal Judaism,

we know. When they state that the first prophet of Allah was Abraham, as founder of Israel the poor Abraham goes belly-up. (And useless to comment that, if I were Jewish, I wouldn't give a damn. Who wants a Founding Father who is ready to slit his own child's throat for the glory of some God?). As for Moses, in the words of the Muslims old Moses becomes an impostor who crosses the Red Sea with Albanian mafia's rubber dinghies. A charlatan who dreams the Promised Land to contend with Arafat. But against those aims Judaism fights tooth and nail. The Catholic Church does not. Of course the Catholic Church knows very well that, according to Muslims, Jesus Christ died of a cold and since then he copulates as a sex-maniac with the virgins Houris in Djanna. It knows very well that Islamic theologians have always lived on that ideological robbery and those grotesque defamations, that they have always judged Christianity as an abortion of Islam. It knows very well that Islamic imperialism has always wanted to conquer the West because the West is the first and true interpreter of Christianity. It knows as well that Islamic colonialism has always tried to subjugate Europe because, besides being rich and full of water, Europe is the cradle of Christianity. A Christianity as manipulated as you want, as distorted as you want, as betrayed as you want, but Christianity.

The Catholic Church also knows very well that, without the crucifix, Charles Martel's French army would have never beaten the Moors at Poitiers. Without the crucifix, Isabella of Castile and Ferdinand of Aragon would have never retaken Andalusia. Nor would have the Normans liberated Sicily from the Saracens. Nor would have Tsar Ivan the Great put an end to almost three centuries of Mongol rule in Russia. It knows as well that without the crucifix we would have never turned down the first and second siege of Vienna. We would have never rejected Süleyman the Magnificent and Kara Mustafa's Ottoman Turks. (Remember what John Sobieski, the heroic king of Poland, shouted to his soldiers during the battle that in 1683 repelled Kara Mustafa? He shouted: «Soldiers! It is not Vienna alone that we must save! It is Christianity, the same idea of Christendom!». And remember what he added soon after? He added: «Soldiers! Let's fight for Our Lady of Czestochowa!». That's right: Our-Lady-of-Czestochowa. The Black Madonna to whom also in the years of Solidarnosc, of the struggle against the colonialism of the Soviet Union, all Poles recurred). And more than anybody the Catholic Church knows that without the crucifix our civilization would not exist. That the roots from which that civilization was born, the roots of Greco-Roman culture, were not passed on to us by the Avicennas and by the Averroës: they were passed on to us seven centuries before by St. Augustine who carried the Greco-Roman culture into Christian theology. Right or wrong, you phony historians and fraudulent academics of the Euro-Arab Dialogue?!? But, more than anybody else, the Catholic Church knows that without the irresistible provocation and the sensational bet we would be speaking a language that does not contain the word Freedom. Liberty. And we would vegetate in a world that, far from rejecting death, sees death as a privilege.

* * *

Yet the Church behaves as if it didn't know. This Catholic Church which behind the screen of «Love-your-enemy-as-you-love-yourself» does not confine itself to running the charitable institutions which welcome Muslim immigrants. Which hide them in their hostels, which get them political asylum and welfare benefits, which block or obstruct their expulsions and in France even sell them convents or churches to transform in mosques... (At Clermont-Ferrand, for example, it was Bishop Dardel who sold to Muslim immigrants the chapel of Saint Joseph Sisters, Alexandre Del Valle tells in

194

his book *La tyrannie de l'Islam*. A chapel they immediately destroyed for the glory of Allah. At Asnières-sur-Seine it was the Catholic Congregation that sold to Muslim immigrants its deconsecrated buildings. Buildings where along with the mosque they constructed a Koran school. In Paris it was the prelate Gilles Couvreur who along with his colleague Christian Delorme supported the foundation of the Islamic Cultural Institute in rue Tanger. An institute backed by Algerian fundamentalist Larbi Kechat. In Lyon it was Cardinal Decourtray who had the Great Mosque built. And here I stop because the list is too long).

This Catholic Church that gets on so well with Islam because not few of its priests and prelates are the first collaborators of Islam. The first traitors. This Catholic Church without whose imprimatur the Euro-Arab Dialogue could neither have begun nor gone ahead for thirty years. This Catholic Church without which the Islamization of Europe, the degeneration of Europe into Eurabia, could never have developed. This Catholic Church that remains silent even when the crucifix gets insulted, derided, expelled from the hospitals. This Catholic Church that never roars against their polygamy and wife-repudiation and slavery. Because in Islam slavery is not a foul stain of the past, my dear priests and bishops and cardinals who preach to love the enemy. In Saudi Arabia it was abolished as late as in 1962. (With words only). In Yemen, the same. And in Sudan, in Mauritania, in other African countries, it still exists. On slavery, in Sudan, the Commission on Human Rights and the American Anti-Slavery Group draft report after report. You don't. In Sudan between 1995 and 2001 Christian Solidarity International succeeded in liberating 47.720 Sudanese Copts. You did not. In the United States every September last Sunday the American Evangelical Churches observe a day's mourning for all the black slaves in Sudan and all the persecuted Christians in the world. You don't. Twelve years ago the then United Nations secretary general Boutros Boutros-Ghali came out in strong condemnation of slavery in Sudan. You didn't. On the contrary, you took the imams to Assisi. You sanctified them on the tomb of St. Francis. Poor St. Francis.

And, this said, let's talk about their allies of the Right and of the Left.

CHAPTER 10

I must clear up a couple of things before I speak of the other two entities which belong to the Triple Alliance. And the first is that when I say Right and Left I do not refer to opposite and irreconcilable entities. One the symbol of regression and one the symbol of progress. I refer to the adverse political sides which, like two soccer teams struggling for the World Cup, chase the ball of Power. Which by reciprocal kicking, elbowing, kneeling and other kinds of perfidiousness try to get it. So they really seem opposite and irreconcilable entities. If you look at them closely, though, you realize that despite the different colours of their shorts and their shirts they are not even two separate entities: they are a homogeneous block. A single team fighting itself. You know why? Because, in the West, the Right no longer exists. I mean the filthy, reactionary, obtuse, feudal Right. The Right which was a symbol of regression. As a concept, that Right vanished with the French Revolution. And, before that, with the American Revolution which transforming the mob into People fixed the principle of Freedom married to Equality. As a reality, it died out with the assertion of the Right arisen from those two revolutions. The enlightened, liberal Right which is defined as the Historical Right. And to understand how true this is, take a look at the most backward and wretched countries of this planet. Apart from Latin America where western civilization is a dream never achieved, all countries placed in the Middle East and Far East and Africa. Muslim countries. Countries subjected for centuries and centuries to Islam. In fact the filthy, reactionary, obtuse, feudal Right can today be found in Islam only. Because today that Right is Islam.

As for the Historical Right, it is by now a memory deleted even from the historians' consciousness. It was a glorious Right. And, in my view, a Right by name not by facts. Aristocratic, yes, but revolutionary. Especially in Italy. Because notwithstanding its kings, its dukes, its counts, its marquises, better yet with them and thanks to them, in Italy it led the Risorgimento. It led the Wars of Independence and even Mazzini, at one point, turned to it. (Letter to His Majesty Carlo Alberto). Even Garibaldi fought with it, respected it. (His entente with King Vittorio Emanuele II, his entrusting to him a Southern Italy already liberated from the foreign usurper). Oh, yes: they were fine men, the men of that Right. Intelligent, courageous, forward-looking, as well as honest. In Italy one was Count Federico Confalonieri. Another one, Marquis Massimo d'Azeglio. Another one, Count Santorre di Santarosa. Another one, the super-Catholic Vincenzo Gioberti. Another one, the noble Carlo Cattaneo. Another one, Camillo Benso Count of Cavour. Another one, Marquis Cosimo Ridolfi. And another one, (that you like it or not), Vittorio Emanuele II. By trade, a king. They gave us liberalism, those fine and honourable men. They gave us Constitutions and Parliaments and democracy, those revolutionaries filled with style. They taught us to live with freedom, they allowed the circulation of ideas most hostile to them. Often, republican and anarchist and socialist ideas. In fact at that time Italians had respect for politics. They loved it with the same passion with which they now love soccer games. In the theatres, in the salons, the taverns, the cafés, they only talked about politics. All right: for half a century such a Right restricted the vote to citizens who were not poor, who could read and write. To women, not even if they were rich and could read and write. Their women, however, did not wear the burkas and the chadors. Among the thousand patriots that Garibaldi led to free Sicily there were several women. With rifles. Skirts down to their feet, whalebone corsets, coquettish hats, and rifles. Only thirty-eight at the beginning. Mainly sisters or sisters-in-law or cousins or mistresses of the Garibaldians. And almost all from the northern cities of Milano, Bergamo, Varese, Pavia, Genova. (Of each of the thirty-eight I have names and last names). But, as soon as landed in Sicily, they more than doubled thanks to dozens of women from the southern cities of Palermo and Catania and Messina. Wearing long skirts, whalebone corsets, coquettish hats, rifles, these too fought side by side with their men. In several battles. And before crossing the straits of Messina, before entering in Calabria, many of them died. Yet in Calabria they multiplied, and by the time Garibaldi reached Naples they were almost two thousand. Along with their husbands and lovers and brothers and sons they achieved other merits also. They helped to evict a papacy which for centuries had exercised the most temporal and masculine power. They helped to eliminate the Papal State and to relegate the Pope inside the few square-meters of Vatican. That Right taught us the concept of «free-Church-in-free-State», of secularism, in short. And finally it taught us the virtues without which any society dies: the love for our homeland, the pride for our national identity, the sense of honour and dignity. As well as the good manners. The respect, the value of quality. Therefore, of merit. Politically Correct nullities and mediocrities always deny merit. They always replace quality with quantity. But it's quality that moves the world. Not quantity, my dears. The world goes on thanks to the few who have quality, value, merit. Not thanks to you who are a lot and stupid. The fact is that struggle wears out, exhausts. And power corrupts. Little by little the Historical Right forgot to be an intelligent Right, a courageous Right, a forward-looking or better a revolutionary Right. At the end of 1800 it let itself be replaced by the newcomers' demagogy and, resting on the past glories, it decayed. It collapsed.

At the beginning of 1900 and for twenty years or so (I'm still speaking about my country, of course) it woke up: true. In fact it was thanks to the aristocratic liberals that we obtained the universal suffrage: not thanks to the socialists. But by now the formerly glorious warrior was a half-blind and half-deaf old lady walking with the stick. One rainy day was enough to make her sneeze, and in 1914 she caught a serious bout of pneumonia: the barbarous, bloody Red Week that syndacalists and socialists and anarchists and republicans let loose in Italy. («What a mistake did we make, what a mistake! How stupid we were, how stupid!» one of the main responsible, the great Socialist Pietro Nenni, said to me over sixty years later). Then, in 1915, she caught an even more serious blow: the First World War. In 1917, she had a stroke which left her half-paralyzed: the Russian Revolution. In 1919 she was attacked by a cancer called Benito Mussolini, in 1921 she took that cancer to the Parliament by accepting him in her electoral pool plus having him elected. And a year later she died. Practically suicidal. Because, despite all the mistakes she had lessened herself with, she could have got rid of that felony. On the contrary, she abetted it. For instance, through her pupil Benedetto Croce who knew a lot about philosophy and Christianity but much less about politics. And, above all, through the not-honourable grandson of Vittorio Emanuele II: Vittorio Emanuele III, the midget king (midget in body and soul) who in October 1922 asked Mussolini to form a government and legitimated Fascism. The fascism that would inspire Nazism.

She died unmourned, the noble old lady who had led the Risorgimento and the Wars of Independence. Who had given us Constitutions and Parliaments, democracy and universal suffrage. She died as a poor harlot. Dishonoured, despised, unmindful of the virtuous things she had taught us. And she never resurrected. Because Mussolini was not a man of the Right. He came from the Socialist Party, from the Red Week. He had been in jail with Pietro Nenni, he had praised the taking of the Winter Palace, he had admired Lenin and Trotsky, he was a man of the Left. His National Fascist Party was not a right-wing party. Like Hitler's National Socialist Party, it was or wanted to be or said to be a left-wing party. His horrible Blackshirts were not aristocrats à la Federico Confalonieri, à la Massimo d'Azeglio, à la Cavour. They were subversive proletarians or bourgeois whose excesses and incoherences have always been the ruin of Western society. (Including America). Not by chance, libraries overflow with books on the red roots of Fascism. The hidden red nature of Fascism. And after half a century the heritage of this reality is so strong that the conservative parties are afraid to admit their conservatism. Even the Thories in England and the Republicans in America pronounce the term Right with a sort of embarrassed caution. As for the Catholics, they refuse it all the way. Oh yes: who uses that term with light heart, nowadays? Who is happy to be identified with the once-noble lady who died dishonoured, despised, unmindful of the virtuous things she had taught? Nowadays the term Right sounds like a discredited word, a retrograde concept, a blasphemy, and also the younger neo-nazis who call themselves Skin-heads prefer to avoid it. The Italian Extreme Right, a Mussolini's residue which resembles the Extreme Left as much as the two soccer-teams I said resemble each other. (The similitude between the Extreme Right and the Extreme Left is a fact that nobody can deny, a reality which portrays and summarizes all the ambiguities of democracy). To acknowledge such truth, it's enough to read the editorial that the 17 of June 1944, when the city of Florence was about to be liberated by the Anglo-Americans, appeared on the last issue of a most mussolinesque magazine of Tuscany: «*Italy and Civilization*». Here it is: «Let Roosevelt and Churchill and their partners know that the most aware Fascists have always recognized Communism as the only force alive and contrary to their own. That they have always identified the real enemy with the plutocratic Britain and the plutocratic America. Never with the Soviet Union, never with Russia. Fascists have always disagreed with a number of points in regard to Communism, yes, but also agreed with many others. To be precise, on what both of them do not want: the old liberal, bourgeois, rotten, capitalistic society». And then: «Roosevelt and Churchill and their partners must realize that should the Axis Rome-Berlin-Tokio miss victory, the majority of Fascists escaped from the scourge would go over to Communism. They would make common cause with it, and this would cross the gap that today separates the two revolutions».

* * *

Who is not there does not rule. Ergo, who today rules in Europe therefore in Italy is not the Right. It is the Left. In all its forms and colours and compromises. In all its open or clandestine alliances. Because, either at the government or at the opposition, either with the physical violence or with the intellectual terrorism, in Italy the Left rules since Mussolini took power: I repeat. And because, soon after the settling of democracy, what the anonymous Fascist had announced on June 17th 1944 became fully true. Black Fascists realized they had always been red Fascists, red Fascists realized they had always been black Fascists, and their obscure bond was restored as if nothing had happened in between. A between which included two decades of dictatorship, a world war, a civil war, an Italy half destroyed, and around a million dead. Or should I say that the bond restored as if it had been a lovers' quarrel or a family misunderstanding?

Apart from very few cases, in fact, a lovers' quarrel or a family misunderstanding had been.

And there are moments when I curse myself for not having understood it earlier: for having let myself be fooled by the two soccer-teams for so long. Dammit, I was only sixteen when that truth began to reveal itself. I well remember the day when my father came home pale with disdain and said: «Communists want to grant amnesty to all the Fascists. Almost nobody opposes, and soon we'll have them wearing red scarfs». (It was 1945). I remember too the Rescue-of-the-Brothers-in-Black-Shirt. A pacification venture that Palmiro Togliatti, at that time the big boss of the Italian Communist Party, had assigned to his most faithful deputies. A dirty affair that in the name of Reconciliation had already been conceived in 1936 but not put into effect because that same year Stalin had ignited the Spanish Civil War. I also remember the beating I received in 1947 at the University of Florence, Faculty of Medicine, at the hands of a Fascist student and a Communist one who did not like my ideas. In perfect symbiosis and synchronization, in fact, both of them kicked me and punched me because I was «pro-American and pro-Zionist». I had not realized, then, the meaning of the rascality, I guess. In 1947 I was so young and naïve. In the Sixties, however, I realized it. I did thanks to Uncle Bruno who before dying had entrusted me with a box full of letters received three decades before. That is, when he was vice-editor in chief of the *Corriere della Sera*. More than letters, threatening warnings sent to him by intellectuals (now belonging to the militant Left) who reproached him for not being a Fascist. One of them came from the renowned Elio Vittorini who in a mussolinesque handwriting admonished: «Fallaci, you are an enemy! You fail to recognize the greatness of our commander!». I realized it even better when in the Seventies I read the book in which the ex-communist Ruggero Zangrandi settled his comrades by revealing the names of the fervent communists who had been fervent fascists. And I understood it even more when Pietro Nenni told me of his last encounter with a certain Beni whose identity I had never heard of. An encounter which had taken place a night of June 1922 on the French Riviera where, after I don't know what international conference, the two had started talking about a disagreement which divided them harshly. Talking and walking along the Croisette they had reached Nice at dawn and here, sad for the good-bye to come, they had finally divided with a heart broken «Goodbye Pietro», «Goodbye Beni». So, overwhelmed by curiosity, at this point of the story I asked: «Excuse me, Nenni, but who was this Beni? I never heard of him!».

Poor me. «You've never heard of him?!? You have never heard of Mussolini?!?» Nenni shouted in disdain. Yes: more than an answer, a shout. «When I say Beni I mean Benito, Benito Mussolini, don't I?!? I say Beni because we were friends, we were fond of each other! Didn't we?!? After the Red Week we even had shared the prison's cell! Hadn't we?!?». Then he calmed down. And to prove how fond they had been of each other he told me that in 1943, when he had been arrested by the SS and sealed inside a train directed to Dachau concentration camp in Germany, Beni had saved his life. He had called Hitler and asked to send him back to Italy to have him exiled on the island of Ponza... He also told me that the 28 of April 1945, when Beni had been executed by a partisan firing-squad, on his newspaper *Avanti!* he had given the news with a cold and dispassionate headline: «Justice is done». But soon after he had shut up himself in a latrine and wept.

* * *

Oh yes. It is a long-term ruler this Left that gave birth to Mussolini then Hitler, and always maintained its bond with their disciples. This Left

208

which has always given trouble with its excesses and ambiguities, its brutalities and duplicities. All right: it has also given something good: I recognize it. In Italy, for instance, it has helped to win vital battles like the referendum for the Republic then for the divorce. It has also understood in time that, if the Communist Party continued to be a satellite of the Soviet Union, the whole of Europe would have become a gulag. Thus it had to accept Nato. But its sins greatly outnumber its merits. And its sins are so many that, if Hell existed, at their death all Communists and Company would plunge headlong into Lucifer's throat. One of those sins (I already said this in *The Rage and the Pride* but I shall never give up repeating what needs to be repeated) concerns its intellectual terrorism. Its presumption and assumption of holding the Truth. Its dogmatism. A dogmatism identical to the one of religions and Churches. «If-you-don't-think-what-I-think, you-are-an-idiot-and-a-delinquent» is the silent slogan that through film-makers and school-teachers and university-professors and intellectuals or pseudo-intellectuals has poisoned two generations and now poisons the third. (Let's be straight. The Red Brigades didn't come out of Cavour's brain: they came out of the belly of the Left. The no-globals and the mendacious pacifists who disseminate the most obtuse illiberalism and the most bullying fascism were not spawned by the Holy Spirit: they were spawned by the Left. And this truth is valid for America too. Doesn't American anti-Americanism originate from its Left?).

However, the most despicable sin with which the Left has sullied itself in the last years is the sin of having fostered and fostering Islamism in Europe. The sin of having contributed, along with the Catholic Church and the noble lady who committed suicide, the Islamization of Europe. If Europe has become Eurabia, the fault mainly belongs to the Left which in all the European countries has behaved and behaves as it does. Now I will demonstrate it to you.

CHAPTER 11

In 1979, that is the year when the mullahs and the ayatollahs ousted the Shah and established the Islamic Republic of Iran, Khomeini dusted down a number of the Koran's Surahs. In particular, those concerning the sexual behaviour of Shia Muslims. On their basis he compiled a set of rules and collected them in a handbook called the «Blue Book». Parts of the «Blue Book» were published by an Italian magazine under the playful title «The Ten Khomeindments», time ago I happened to read them again, and... One says: «If a woman has carnal relations with her future husband, after marrying her the husband has the right to demand the annulment of the marriage». Another says: «Marriage with one's own sister or one's own mother or one's own mother-in-law is a sin». Another says: «A man who has had sexual relations with his own aunt cannot marry her daughter, that is, his cousin». Another says: «A Muslim woman cannot marry a heretical man and a Muslim man cannot marry a heretical woman. However he can enter into concubinage with Jewish and

Christian women». Another says: «If a father has three daughters and wants to give one of them in marriage, at the wedding cerimony he must specify which daughter he is giving». And another: «A marriage may be annulled if after the wedding the groom discovers that the bride is lame or blind or afflicted by leprosy or by other skin diseases». Another (even more appalling because it refers to the nine years old brides, the age at which a Muslim girl can be married): «If a man marries a minor who has reached the age of nine and if during the defloration he immediately breaks the hymen, he cannot enjoy her any longer». Another (as much appalling because it entails that a girl may be deflored before she is nine): «If a widowed or repudiated wife has not reached the age of nine, she may remarry soon after the widowhood or the repudiation without waiting for the prescribed four months and ten days. She may do so even if recently she has had intimate relations with the first husband». Another: «If a wife does not obey her husband and is not always available for his pleasure, if under some pretext she does not give him joy, the husband must not give her food or clothing or lodging». Another: «The mother and the daughter and the sister of a man who has had anal relations with another man may not marry the latter. But if the latter has had or is having anal relations with an acquired relative, the marriage remains valid». Lastly: «A man who has had sexual relations with an animal, such as a sheep, may not eat its meat. He would commit sin».

I read them again and more than nausea they gave me a sort of malady. Because I remembered that in 1979 the Italian or rather European Left had fallen in love with Khomeini just as now it has fallen in love with Bin Laden and Saddam Hussein and Arafat. Thus I said to myself: am I wrong or the Left is the first daughter of secularism and should be super laic? Thus, how can it possibly speak of revolution when it refers to Khomeini and Khomeinism? The Left speaks of progress. For a century it has been singing hymns to Progress, to Improvement, to the Sun of the Future. Thus, how can it possibly be fornicating with the most backward and reactionary ideology on Earth?!? The Left was born and grew in the West. It is western. It belongs to the most evolved civilization in history. Thus, how can it possibly identify with a world in which you have to be told that marrying your mother is wrong and eating the sheep you keep as your mistress is a sin?!? How can it possibly sing the praises of a world in which a girl can be widowed or repudiated at the age of nine or before?!? Then my sort of malady became an obsession, and I started asking: «Do you understand, can you understand, why the Left is on the side of Islam?». Well... Some answered: «Because the Left is pro-Third World, anti-American, anti-Zionist. Islam is also so. In Islam the Left sees what the Red Brigaders call their natural-ally». Others answered: «Because with the collapse of the Soviet Union and the rise of capitalism in its former States and in China, the Left has lost the old points of reference. Ergo, it clings to Islam as to a lifebelt». Or: «It's obvious. In Europe the real proletariat no longer exists, and a Left without a proletariat is like a shopkeeper with no goods. So in the Islamic proletariat the Left has found the merchandise it needs for selling: a future reservoir of votes». But, although all the answers contained an indisputable truth, none of them took account of the reasoning my question was based upon. I continued to torment myself, and this lasted until I realized that my question was wrong.

It was wrong because it came from a residue of respect for the Left I had known as a child. The Left of my grandparents, of my parents, of my dead comrades, of my youth's utopias. The Left that ceased to exist half a century ago. It was wrong also because it came from the political solitude in which I have always lived. A political solitude which at that time included the one given to me by moral and intellectual desert of the phony heroes in whom I had believed as a youngster. Justice-and-freedom. Liberal-socialism. And so on. But above all it was wrong because the reasonings or rather the premises on which I based my interrogative were wrong. First premise, my illusion that the Left would be laic. I mean secular. Though the daughter of secularism, (besides a secularism begotten by liberalism and consequently not consonant with dogmatism), the Left is not laic. Whether it dresses in red or black or pink or green or white or in all the colours of the rainbow, the Left is confessional. Ecclesiastic. Because it derives from an ideology of religious character. That is, because it appeals to an ideology which claims to possess the Truth. On one side, the Good. On the other, the Evil. On one side, the Sun of the Future. On the other, the Darkness. On one side, the comrades. The blessed ones, the faithful. On the other, the infidels or rather infidel-dogs. The Left is a Church. And not a Church similar to the Church which came out of Christianity, thus open to free-will. A Church similar to Islam. Like Islam it considers itself sanctified by a God who is the custodian of the Truth. Like Islam it never acknowledges its faults and its errors, it considers itself infallible and never apologizes. Like Islam it demands a world at its own image, a society built on the verses of its Prophet. Like Islam it enslaves its own followers. It intimidates them, it makes them feel stupid even when they are intelligent. Like Islam it does not accept different opinions and if you think differently it despises you. It denigrates you, it punishes you. Like Islam, in short, it is illiberal. Autocratic, totalitarian, even when it plays the game of democracy. For Christsake, isn't it revealing that ninety-five percent of the Western people converted to Islam come from the Left or the red-black Extreme Left? A ninety-five percent of the Muslims naturalized Italian or French or Spanish or German or British or Scandinavian, by the way. (The skunk who doesn't want the crucifix in our schools or hospitals and who invites his brothers to-go-and-die-with-Fallaci, for instance, comes from the red-black Extreme Left. His buddy, and co-author of the libel which asks to kill me, has even been in prison for connivance with the Red Brigades). Like Islam, finally, the Left is anti-West. And the cause why it is anti-West can be summarized with a passage of *The Road to Serfdom*: one of the important essays left to us by Friedrich Hayek, the Austrian economist who in the Thirties flew from Vienna and took refuge in England.

«It is not only the principles of Adam Smith and Hume and Locke and Milton which are being abandoned. It is also the bedrock of the civilization developed by the Greeks and the Romans and

Christianity. Meaning, the western civilization. What is being relinquished is not only the liberalism of the 18th and 19th centuries, that is the liberalism which completed that civilization» it says. «It is the individualism which, thanks to Erasmus of Rotterdam and Montaigne and Cicero and Tacitus and Pericles and Thucydides, the western civilization has inherited. In other words, the concept itself of individualism which through the teachings imparted to us by the philosophers of classical antiquity then of Christianity then of Renaissance then of the Enlightenment have made us what we are. Socialism is based on collectivism. Collectivism denies individualism. And anyone who denies individualism denies western civilization».

*   *   *

Assumption: if Hayek is wrong and I am wrong, if the similarity between the Left and Islam does not exist, tell me why it was precisely during the governments of the red and green and pink and white and rainbow Left that the Triple Alliance delivered my country to Islam. Tell me why it was precisely in those years that the Islamic invasion strengthened, stabilized. Tell me why the huge majority of immigrants was (still is) Muslim.

217

(At least two million, up today. That is, 3.6% of the Italian population. In Center and North Italy, 4.6%: a percentage which equals and sometimes outstrips the one of the most invaded British and French and German cities).

Tell me also why it was precisely in those years that their mosques multiplied and began to produce false passports, false Residence Permits, plus Al Qaeda material. And why terrorists began to be recruited by the imams to be sent to Bosnia and to Chechnya and to Afghanistan. Tell me why it was precisely in those years that police forces went soft, cops and prefects started to treat immigrants with deferential courtesy, and the Carabinieri were ordered not to react when insulted or threatened by them. Tell me why it was precisely in those years that magistrates of the Left started to protect the sons of Allah by favouring the arrival of their families, by impeding their expulsion, by turning a blind eye to cases of polygamy. And not infrequently by releasing on the grounds of «procedural-irregularities» those found in possession of firearms and explosives. Such magistrates are so numerous, by now, that while reviewing the appeal of an Albanian convicted for bringing a sixteen year-old prostitute to Italy, the Court of Cassation found the way to criticize the Center-Right government and to praise the former Center-Left government which «had-laid-the-foundations-of-civil-coexistence». (More or less what happens in France, in England, in Germany, in Spain, where being concerned with public order is «a unilateral interpretation of European laws»).

Tell me also why, just then, so many unacceptable episodes began to arise all over Italy. The case of the Cuneo's High School where the teachers declared the first day of Ramadan as a Day's Holiday, to begin with. The case of the La Spezia High School where, in order to please a Muslim student temporarily camped in the area, a leftist teacher removed the crucifix from the classroom. The case of Como Elementary School where the whole body of pacifist female teachers rejected the Mayor who, dressed as Santa Claus, had arrived carrying a large bag of Christmas presents. (And too bad if the children burst into tears: «We want the presents»). «Dressing up as Santa Claus and offering those Christmas toys was a politically incorrect act. Christmas irritates the Muslim pupils and must not be considered a religious festivity» the stupid women declared to the press. Or the case of the Puglia Elementary School where another female teacher banned the Nativity Crib. And too bad if there too the children burst into tears, cried «We want the Crib». (For this the female teacher received the congratulations of the Democratic Left mayor). Or the case of Val d'Aosta kindergarten where the parents of the only Muslim child of the village informed the director that they did not appreciate the Christmas carols sung in class. Particularly, one that said: «You come down from the stars, our dear King of Heaven»... And again: don't forget that I provide these examples because such things happen in Italy and are familiar to me. In any country of Europe it happens exactly the same. (But now let me tell you the case which recently took place in Florence: the city ruled by the Left since more than half a century. I mean the case known as «The Italian way to infibulation»).

* * *

You know what infibulation is, don't you? It is the mutilation that Muslims impose on their little girls to prevent them, when grown, (or even before, if they marry at the age of nine), from enjoying the sexual act. It is the female castration that Muslims impose in twenty-eight countries of Islamic Africa. And, because of which, every year two million young girls die of sepsis or loss of blood. (The figure is given by the World Health Organization). And you know what it consists of? It consists in removing the clitoris, that is the genital organ located in the upper part of the vulva, and in cutting off the labia minora then sewing the labia majora and leaving only a tiny slit to allow urination. An atrocity usually carried out by the girl's mother with scissors or a knife then with a normal needle and a normal thread. That is, without sterilized instruments and without any form of anaesthesia. In Europe the practice is prohibited by the Criminal Code, and in Italy the Parliamentary Commission on Justice and Social Affairs has drafted a bill which permits to issue on whoever practises it a penalty going from six to twelve years of prison. But apparently determined to save the principle, not to abolish it, early this year the Somali gynaecologist who directs the Maternity Section of Florence's main hospital proposed a compromise consisting of a «pinprick» instead of the clitoris removal. «It's a matter of surgery that only requires a momentary wound: a soft-infibulation which makes it possible to preserve the ritual and celebrate all the same what for Muslim women is a sort of baptism» he said. He could because he had gotten the imprimatur of the Democratic Left president of the Tuscany region and of his hangman's-assistants. Among them, a doctor who collects the most incredible number of public ranks in Tuscany and who is an exponent of the Bioethic Commission plus a drafter of the Medical Professional Ethics Code.

Yet do you know what was the statement released by this presumed Hyppocrates to whom I wouldn't entrust the medication of an ingrowing nail? It was: «Questions of professional ethics should be put aside to respect this very ancient ritual. I am in favour of the Somali colleague's project and I personally recommend to put it in effect». But there is more. Because when a congresswoman of the Center-Right brought the matter before Parliament and speaking of a «barbaric custom» called for the intervention of the entire political world, her female counterparts of the Center-Left invited her to shut up her mouth. Only when the battle exploded on a national scale was the soft-infibulation project rejected. Which in no way rules out my wish of addressing an angry letter to the protagonists of the iniquitous story.

(Letter to the not-magnificent protagonists of the iniquitous story. «Sirs, I won't bother explaining to you that ethics is based on principles. That principles cannot be circumvented with compromises or political tricks. That therefore the point is not to make infibulation less painful or less dangerous. The point is to prohibit it. To prevent it. To punish it. No matter how it is performed. Given the fact that you put principles aside, that to principles you prefer rituals, I will not even bother reminding you that infibulation is the equivalent of castration. Which means, the other "very-ancient-ritual" which turns roosters into capons, bulls into oxen, men into eunuchs. That in the West castration was practised for many centuries in order to obtain angelical treble-voices, and that in the 18th century the Enlightenment succeeded in having it abolished with the word "barbarity". You already know that, I guess. For my own pleasure, however, I will bother to remind you that there are two forms of castration. One bloody and one bloodless. Called "soft". The bloody one is basically carried out in the way usually infibulation is carried out in Islam. That is, with not sterilized scissors and knives. It consists in removing the testicles with the same procedure which removes the little girls' clitoris. And, to remove the testicles, each testicular cord is gripped in round-edged pincers. The flow of blood is stopped, and zac! Zac! Out they go. A procedure less painful than the cutting-off of the clitoris and of the labia minora plus the sewing-up of the labia majora. But very unpleasant all the same... The bloodless or soft castration consists, instead, in getting rid of the testicles without removing them. That is, atrophying them with chemicals. In both cases, though, the effects are devastating. Physically, psychologically, neurologically, mentally and emotionally. In the first case as well as in the second, in fact, the castrato grows obese. He loses his beard and head hair and body hair. He forgets his sexual desires. He falls prey to violent bouts of hysteria and precocious senility. Worse: his intelligence extinguishes. It degenerates into idiocy or madness, and who cares for the angelical treble voice which trills the praises of the Lord or the Violetta's solos of *La Traviata*. As a human being he is finished. To stay alive he must resign himself to being a eunuch in a harem of Yemen or Sudan. In the name of fair play, I therefore express the wish that all of you end up as eunuchs in a harem of Yemen or Sudan. All of you: yes. Castrated, obese, bald, hysterical, brain-softened. Men no more men. Not only: in the name of the Muslim little girls infibulated or to be infibulated with scissors or a pin, and by appointment of the Muslim women who thank me and wish me well, I volunteer as executioner of your castration. But not with the "soft" method, of course. With the round-edged pincers. Zac, zac! Zac, zac! Zac, zac! Out they go». End of the letter).

* * *

If Hayek is wrong and I am wrong, tell me finally why, just during the years when the Italian Left was officially ruling, in Italy Muslim immigrants increased with the most inexorable crescendo. By the end of 1996, from 1.6 to 1.9% of the population. By 1997, to 2.2%. By 2001, to 2.4%. (Not counting the illegal ones). Tell me why it was just then that their so-called family-reunifications rose with the same speed. (Forty-five percent of the new arrivals were wives who had remained behind, and it was then that foreign births began to multiply at dramatic rates). Also tell me why in our prisons the number of foreigner inmates multiplied at the rate of 10 then 20 then 30%. And why in 1998 the number of the clandestine sons of Allah grew by 13% compared to 1997. In 1999, by 15.8% compared to 1998. In 2000, by 23% compared to 1999. And why their expulsions turned into a farce. And why in 1999 fifty-six thousand expelled by injunction did not leave and were not arrested. And why the leftist majority passed a law which did not consider an offence for illegal immigrants the refusal of showing their documents and even revealing their country of origin. And why the delirium of an anti-Americanism which identifies with anti-Westernism (I prefer to call it anti-Occidentalism) bloomed directly proportionate to the multi-culturalism that the Left preached only for the Muslims. (Never for the Buddhists or the Hindus or the Confucians and so on). Tell me why it was just then that the red and black extremists

realized to be two peas in the same pod and together they started bellowing «God smash America».
Together they began shouting against the «reactionary plutocracies of the West». A slogan, the former, which was very similar to the one that during
the Second World War the Black-Shirts of Mussolini used to impose by decorating their jacket-
lapels with a badge which said: «God damn the
British». A terminology, the latter, identical to the
one that Mussolini had launched the 10th of June
1940 for his declaration of war. «Italians! We take
the field against the reactionary plutocratic democracies of the West».

Which is not all.

CHAPTER 12

It is not all because it is not only the Triple Alliance's soldiery, I mean the mob of the school-teachers and parlamentarians and clerics with the rainbow scarfs around their neck, which dispense the poison of the anti-Americanism I define anti-Occidentalism. It also is the soldiery of the mendacious media. The so-called «independent» newspapers and televisions and radios and show-business, I mean the journalists and the actors and the singers who are the best accomplices of anti-Occidentalism. The real traitors of the West. Those who more than anybody else administer the ultimate brainwashing of our society. I have before me the front pages of the newspapers that on December 15th 2003 announced the capture of Saddam Hussein. I choose the *Corriere della Sera*. And alongside the well-known picture of the defeated Saddam with a Marine medical officer examining his mouth then removing fleas from his hair, what do I see? A ferocious anti-American message expressed by a cartoon worthy of the Mussolinian «God damn the British» or of the ca-

227

ricatures that during the Second World War the German and Italian press divulged to mock Winston Churchill and Franklin Delano Roosevelt. In fact it depicts a loathsome George W. Bush who standing on a pedestal like Julius Caesar wears a broad laurel wreath on his head, and raises two right-hand fingers to claim victory. Sitting on his shoulders, a minuscule Berlusconi who pokes his face inside the laurel wreath and splays his fingers in turn. And where is the ferocious anti-American better yet anti-Western message paged up? Right inside the text of an article with which a brilliant and honest academic praises the lesson in civility that with this bloodless capture America has given to Europe. Because towards Saddam Hussein who used to kill his own people, to torture them, to asphyxiate them, to bury them alive, but who now is vanquished, the reader feels a kind of pity. Almost a sympathy. For the victor on the pedestal, on the contrary, he feels an instinctive antipathy. A kind of repulsion. As a consequence, he will read the article written by the brilliant and honest academic with a raised eyebrow then will concentrate on the cartoon.

I watch too, or rather I watch again, the news broadcast the same day by the Italian State Television. A broadcasting I happened to record. And what do I see? The New York correspondent who, savouring the word «empire», informs his audience that at the National Building Museum in Washington the United States have crowned Bush as «emperor». As «head of the American Empire». Well, since the National Building Museum is not Capitol Hill and the United States are not a country ruled by kings or emperors, I conduct a quick investigation and guess what I find out. That Bush has gone to the museum for the annual Charity Concert organized by the Children's National Medical Center, that there he has given a little sermon on Christmas kindness and has received a mild round of applause. Without being awarded. Not even granted a symbolic tin medal. Yet, I am sure, many Italians believed that America had actually paid imperial homage to Bush. That he had been carried in triumph like a Julius Caesar who is about to don the purple robes and strike coins with his own image. So in the mind of those who besides TV news saw the ferocious message, anti-Americanism (better yet anti-Occidentalism) inflated still more. Subjection to Islam, the same.

A brainwashing which is at the same time crude and refined, ignorant and educated. The brainwashing characterized by smart advertising techniques. And on what are those techniques based upon? On emblematic clichés. On photographs, punchlines, slogans. On eye-catching graphics, layouts which settle the wrong message in the right place. On visual impacts, in short, on epidermic and irrational shocks. Never on concepts, on reasonings which induce people to ponder upon an idea or an event. Take the «Voyage-of-Hope»: a slogan now more widespread and incessant than the mendacious Napoleon's «Liberté-Egalité-Fraternité». Take the pictures of the Muslim immigrants who try to reach Sicily with rotten boats and sink. Take the heart-rending interview, the tear-jerking article on them. What is a tear-jerking article? Simple. It's the story of the Iraqi or Palestinian child (never an Israeli one) who gets killed or maimed because of Sharon or Bush. (Never because of Arafat or Bin Laden or Saddam Hussein). It is also the story of the stupid Marine who in defiance of regulations marries the Muslim girl living in Baghdad then leaks military secrets to her. So the cruel US army sends him back to the States, asks him to divorce, and the poor Muslim girl falls sick with sorrow. It is also the story of the intrepid Nigerian who walks across the Sahara to come to Italy. Who eroically defies the marauders, acrosses the desert in the baking sun, marches for days along the Old Slave Route. And woe betide you if you remind that journalist that the slaves were sold by Muslim tribes, not by us. That the slave trade was run by Muslim merchants not by us, that the Old Slave Route was closed down by the French and the British and the Belgian colonialists, not by the Koran's disciples. It is also the story of Ahmed or Khaled or Rashid who has lived illegally in Italy for five years. Who in the end has been expelled by a merciless cop. Who now is back in Tunisia or Algeria or Morocco where he hasn't even a girl. Worse: he has never kissed a girl. To kiss her, he has to marry her. To marry her, he has to have money. To have money he must go back to Italy. Ergo, he lives in the dream of landing a second time in the Promised Land and stands on the Tunisian or Algerian or Moroccan beach where he obsessively repeats: «I'll go back. Italian laws cannot stop me, I'll go back». Then he sniffs the wind from Sicily. He fills his lungs with it, he murmurs: «I breathe the scent of your oranges, of Italy. This wind brings me the scent of Italy».

Indeed the tear-jerking article is usually a story well chosen and well written. An elegant journalism on the verge of literature, a work of seduction and persuasion. A science that instead of reason uses sentiment. In fact the brainwashing you get is actually an emotional one. An impact identical to the impact exercised by the cartoons, by the Muslim immigrants' photos, by the Voyage-of-Hope slogan. Or should I say more profound and effective than that because, by touching your heart, it neutralizes your defences. It switches off logic and replaces it with the pity you feel when you see Saddam Hussein disoriented, humiliated, vanquished by a medical officer who removes fleas from his head. It also lights up an uneasiness that at first you don't know how to define, but then you do and a shudder runs down your spine. For heaven's sake, you think, I'm a westerner. I don't wear a burka or a djellabah, I don't belong to an uncompassionate world, to an unmerciful God who compares infidel-dogs with camels and monkeys and pigs. I belong to a civilized, advanced society. To a world which recognizes the free-will, the sense of responsibility, the respect for your neighbour even if the neighbour is a bastard. But despite knowing that Ahmed-Khaled-Rashid has never uttered the fine words the journalist attributes to him, (I-breathe-the-scent-of-Italy, this-wind-brings-me-the-scent-of-Italy), despite knowing that in all probability Ahmed-Khaled-Rashid is a no-good and maybe an Al Qaeda footsoldier, despite suspecting that he has kissed many girls and probably put them pregnant too, you feel responsible for his fate. You feel the temptation to save him, such a temptation that you would like to rent a motorboat, get him to Sicily and call Berlusconi to say: «Sir, could you please find some room for this unfortunate Muslim who loves the scent of Italy and has never kissed a girl? Better: could you please let him marry one of your daughters? Better: could you please grant him the right to vote at once? Better still: could you have him elected as a senator or as the mayor of Rome? Yessir, as the mayor of Rome. And never mind if he will turn all churches into mosques. Never mind if he will turn all domes into minarets».

You react, in short, as I reacted the evening when the great-grandson of the midget king, the scion of the family that delivered Italy to Mussolini, was interviewed on TV and in a heart-rending voice he moaned: «Oh, what would I give to eat a pizza in Naples!». It wasn't much of a line, I agree. It didn't have the poetry of «I-breathe-the-scent-of-Italy» etcetera. As an argument and as a request to be forgiven for the sins of his forefathers, it also seemed very weak. But *chacun dit ce qu'il peut*, everyone says what he can, Cavour used to sigh when he was told about the bullshits pronounced by the scions of the Royal House. And belonging to a civilized world, a world which asks to respect your neighbour even if he is a bastard, I commented: «Poor wretch. What has he to do with the sins of his forefathers? Let him go to Naples and eat his fucking pizza». I mean, yes: in reading that stuff, you let yourself being infected by

233

the brainwashing. Soon after, though, you realize that your conscience has been taken in. That you too have been fooled, mocked, put to sleep. You wake up and see the mosques which silence the ding-dong of the bells, which aim to wipe out the churches as in 1453 the Ottoman troops wiped out Constantinople's cathedral of Santa Sofia. You see the bullies in djellabah who invade the squares of Turin and the streets of Milano to pray and stop the traffic. You see the Drafts of Agreement which with their brazen and fraudulent demands pretend to rummage inside our libraries, boss our archeological sites, take possession of our art-works. You see the shameless imams who preach the Jihad and spit on our dead, on our young men slaughtered at Nassiriyah. You see the letter of the good businessman who wrote you: «I have four Muslim workers and I'm scared. Guess what would happen if they came to know that my grandmother was a Jew». You see the friend who two Easters ago sent toys and chocolate eggs to the five children of the Tunisian woman living next to your house in Tuscany. Toys and eggs that she returned with these words: «I don't want my children to have your Easter presents. For us Muslims your Easter is an insult, a garbage». You see the imam of Carmagnola who was about turning the old Piedmontese town into an exclusively Mu-

234

slim city, you see his Italian wife who says: «We shall conquer you by producing children. You're in zero growth, we're doubling every day. We'll prevail, Rome will become the capital of Islam». You see all the repulsive things I have been talking about till now and you get furious. You convince yourself that the twice invader Ahmed-Khaled-Rashid, or whatever his name is, does not want to come back to Italy in order to eat an innocent pizza like the scion of the midget king. He wants to come back to eat our homeland. So the scent he speaks of is not a scent of oranges. Still less the scent of a girl to kiss. It's the scent of our identity to annul, of our freedom to suppress, of our civilization to destroy. And you shout: «Dear-Ahmed-Khaled-Rashid or whatever your name is, of that scent very little is left. Thanks to your countrymen and mine, most of it has become stench. But the little that is left does not belong to you. Thus stay far from us. Go and find a girl to kiss in the scentless better yet stinking Mecca».

* * *

The trouble is that deflecting him to Mecca is no use anymore. Even without considering the Policy of the Womb preached by Boumedienne,

235

the battle is lost. (Not the war as yet, but the battle for sure). And not even the intrepid Sobieski with his Madonna of Czestochowa could undo the damage which has been done. Look around, think over. Fadhal Nassim, the twenty-four year-old Tunisian who last August blew himself up with the UN head office in Baghdad, used to live in Eurabia. To be precise, on the French Riviera where he pushed drugs between Nice and Menton but often he came to Italy where his brother Saadi is known to the Anti-terrorism Police of Milano. And since the patriarch of the Nassim family runs a mosque in Tunis where he says «I-hope-all-my-sons-will-die-as-martyrs», it is legitimate to suspect that Saadi does not stay in Milano to recite Paternosters and Ave Marias. Yet the Anti-terrorism policemen don't arrest him, don't expel him, don't even bother him. Know why? Because, though realizing that he is an Al Qaeda man, they have no irrefutable proof of it. Should they arrest him or expel him or watch him too closely, some rainbow scarved judge would immediately stop them. Some leftist congressman or congresswoman would immediately intercede in his favour and some tear-jerking journalist would immediately intervening with a tear-jerking article which tells his martyrdom...

We live in democracy by name not by fact, remember? A weak and devitalized democracy

where citizens like me may be put on trial, persecuted, denigrated, practically condemned to death,
but the sons of Allah enjoy a special treatment.
Lofti Rihani, the twenty-six year-old Tunisian who
last October blew himself up outside the Hotel
Rashid in Baghdad, enjoyed that treatment too.
Lofti Rihani lived in Milano like Saadi. He lodged
in a building closely watched by the special units
of Anti-terrorism Police. The Bligny Avenue building, the ghastly building where seven hundred
sons of Allah (most of them illegal) cram inside
two hundred fifty tiny apartments. Well: according to the patrols' reports, Lofti Rihani's successor (I mean Saadi) assiduously frequents the mosque which enrols terrorists by dozens. Yet our
authorities never let special units put their hands
on him. Exactly what happens with the other seven hundred. Special units know everything about
them: at what time they get up, at what time they
go to bed, what canteens they eat in, what prosti-
tutes (usually Brazilian transvestites) they copulate with. They know their mobile-phone's numbers, whom they call, whom they are called by.
What they tell, what they are told, what they
spend to tell and to be told. (A lot of money. But
their financier, Al Qaeda, is not stingy on the expensive conversations). Our special units also know in
what sites or companies or houses they work or

don't work, in what markets they do their shopping. Exclusively markets run by North Africans because Al Qaeda forbids them to spend money in westerners' shops. «Giving money to the pigs is a sin» says the rule. (And don't ask who the «pigs» are... They are the Western morons who host them. The good citizens who support them with their welfare benefits. Who cure them in their hospitals free of charge. Who educate their children in their schools and their universities. Don't ask why nobody ever touches them and why Eurabia continues to be an Al Qaeda headquarters. Their preferred outpost, the base from which they most frequently depart to spread death. If you do, you are called a racist. A xenophobe, an instigator to hate).

I've put aside a newspaper reporting a telephone call intercepted in Milano last November. A conversation between the brother of a recently deceased kamikaze, a certain Sajd, and his mother. One of the mothers who in order to get their hands on the money (namely the «damage-award») urge their sons to blow themselves up. One of the vultures who at the news of the accomplished death laugh with joy and thank Allah. Sajd's brother speaks from Milano. Sajd's mother from a city of the Maghreb. And here is the transcript. Sajd's brother: «Mammy, congratulations for Sajd!

Our Sajd has become a martyr!». Sajd's mother: «Happy news, happy news!». Sajd's brother: «Are you really happy, mammy?». Sajd's mother: «Happy, yes, joyous! Have no fear, my liver. (Sic). You must fear only Allah. It is Allah who shows us the righteous way». Sajd's brother: «Here in Italy everyone admires him and envies him, mammy». Sajd's mother: «Here too there are so many people who congratulate! Allah is great. Let's thank Allah. Allah akbar, Allah akbar!». Then Sajd's brother informs Sajd's mother that one of Sajd's admirers in Italy wants to send her a present of eight thousand euros or dollars. (Again: «damage-award»). The fact is that he is about to get married, and half of those eight thousand euros would help to fix up his house. So: «Mammy, couldn't we go halves?». Sajd's mother hesitates, marks time, procrastinates. Apparently she's tight-fisted. Not prepared to give discounts. All of a sudden, however, she answers: «All-right». And the groom-to-be asks her to send him «in the usual way» the papers he needs to get married. In «the usual way» because he has problems with the Italian State. (An illegal immigrant, for sure). She agrees and, to reassure her, Sajd's brother concludes: «Anyway, don't worry, mammy. Don't be alarmed. With my marriage everything will be all right. I am going to marry an Italian».

*   *   *

Of course: an Italian. A good Italian girl
(isn't so that we say?) who will enable him to become a citizen, a voting citizen, a citizen with all
the rights of the real citizens, in no time at all.
Who will bear him lots of children to bring up in
the Koran. Who has certainly already converted
to Islam and already wears at least the chador.
And who doesn't know, or doesn't comprehend,
that the four thousand euros or dollars to fix up
the house where she will live are dripping with
blood. Her people's blood. Who doesn't realize
that her homeland, her world, is burning. That it
is going up in flames with its past, its present, its
future. Troy-burns, Troy-burns. And by the way:
is there anyone who feels like extinguishing such
fire, such arson?

EPILOGUE

The recidivous heresy is accomplished and Mastro Cecco (this time Mastra Cecca) prepares to go, to return, to the stake. Not the stake, the burning, of our civilization. (A burning which is already under way). Her own, her personal one. She is so prepared, poor Mastra Cecca, that she can already imagine the details of the auto-da-fé with which Sigrid Hunke's pupils will celebrate the punishment. (An auto-da-fé with a compelling ceremony, never modified over the centuries). She imagines, I imagine it, in Florence. In Santa Croce square where in 1328 Messer Jacopo da Brescia burned me when I was Mastro Cecco, and where this time his role is played by a Nobel Prize who half a century ago was a Mussolini's Black Fascist but now is a Red Fascist of the Extreme Left. Look with me: the square is full. It overflows with a crowd of excited rabble that does not understand who the heretic is. What she wants, which side of the barricade she is on. It only knows that her death will be atrocious, and this amuses all of them even more than a soccer game. Full are also the balconies requisitioned by the ladies and the knights of the Triple Alliance. Parliamentarians, Euro-parliamentarians, extra-parliamentarians, party leaders, pacifists, bishops, archbishops, cardinals, mullahs, ayatollahs, imams, newspaper editors, high officials of the State Television. Each of them, waving a rainbow flag or a rainbow scarf. And in the meantime the bells sound the death-knell.

They had been silent for an eternity or what seemed an eternity, the bells. Multi-culturalism had silenced them out of respect for the Prophet. But, as today their sound must be the one of the death-knell, the Mayor of Florence (Democratic Left party) has granted a special permit. Their dong-dong is grim. Not solemn: grim. Because it mixes with the ugly voice of the muezzins who bay their inevitable Allah-akbar. And in this scenery the procession defiles. The heart of the event. To lead it, the Dominican friars who advance raising the banners with the motto «Iustitia et Misericordia», Justice and Mercy, surmounted by an olive branch. A branch identical to the one which symbolizes the current grouping of the Italian Left, meaning the Olive Tree. (I found the invaluable information on page 78 of *L'Inquisizione in Toscana*). Behind the

Dominican friars, the Combonian friars who dispense the «Residence Permits in the Name of God» to illegal immigrants. Then, the no-globals with their elegant white overalls designed by the Politically Correct stylists. Then the Palestinian and Tunisian, Algerian, Moroccan, Syrian, Egyptian, Nigerian, Pakistani, Saudi, Iraqi, Somali, Jordanian aspirant kamikazes who proceed with the explosives around their waists and the mothers who display a fat cheque. The «damage-award» in dollars. Then the Grand Inquisitor who advances with a very voguish keffiah and riding an Iraqi thoroughbred horse. This time, not Fra' Accursio but the Bishop of Caserta. Behind the Bishop of Caserta, the Cudgeler Friars led by the defunct sheikh Ahmed Yassin in his wheelchair. Then, Mussolini's chubby granddaughter who amidst crowd's laughters struts holding a placard which says: «Grandfather's Party». Behind her, the Howling Friars of the Anti-Imperialist Front: the Franciscans of Assisi who tenderly hold the rainbow scarved magistrates' hands. Then the soft-infibulists who obese and bald and castrated, thus reduced to eunuchs, trill Violetta's solo. «Amami Alfreeedooo! Amami quanto io t'amooo!». Finally, the tear-jerking journalists and the leftist Monte de' Paschi Bank's cartoonist who delighting for my impending martyrdom declaims the Requiem Aeternam. And, following all of them, Mastra Cecca. That is I who barefoot, worn out, disfigured by lashes and other scourges as well as bundled up in a burka-like sanbenito (rendered even more ridiculous by a conical mitre), move on like a ghost. Beside me, the Executor of Justice who this time is not Messer Jacopo da Brescia. It's the Red Brigades' self-proclaimed leader: the female who plays the European proletariat's warrior, now released from prison for good behaviour. And who, after tying my body to the stake, asks me (it makes part of the procedure) which religion I wish to die in. Because, if I answer «in-the-Roman-Catholic-Apostolic-Church» or better still «in-the-Religion-of-Islam», she may exercise the mercy alluded to by the Dominican friars' banners «Justice and Mercy». A mercy which consists in strangling me then burning me when I am already dead. If I answer (as I shall) with a raspberry, instead, she will burn me alive.

I imagine all this without really believing in it, of course. The auto-da-fé is a politically debatable matter for the now refused death-penalty as well for the crucifixes and the bells: two symbols scarcely appreciated by the Euro-Arab Dialogue. Summary and stealthy executions are much more in fashion. The pistol-shot fired by the pro-Iraqi pacifist, for instance. The bomb blown up by Sajd's brother who thereby can collect the full amount of eight thousand euros or dollars. In such case, though, the Triple Alliance should be forced to condemn the act. So would the European Union and the Human Rights' UN charlatan Doudou Diène and all other enemies of mine. The President of the Italian Republic would be even compelled to attend my funerals (State Funerals). A possibility to be ruled out because in my books I have not been benevolent with his benevolence towards the invaders. Ergo, I think that for me the punishment will continue to take place in the way it takes place since four years. That is the way explained by Alexis de Tocqueville at the conclusion of his undying work on democracy.

* * *

In dictatorial or absolutist regimes, Tocqueville explains, despotism strikes the body. Grossly and murderously. That is, putting it in chains then torturing it or suppressing it in various ways. Beheadings, hangings, shootings, stonings, Inquisition stakes etcetera. In so doing it ignores the soul which can rise intact over the mangled flesh and transform the victim into a hero. In the inanimate democracies, (I call them weak and devitalized democracies), in the inertly democratic regimes, despotism ignores the body and attacks the soul. Because it is the soul that it wants to put in chains, to torture, to suppress. In fact its victims are never told as in absolutist regimes: «Either you think as I do or you die». They are told: «You choose. You're free not to think or to think as I do. And if you think differently to me, I shall not punish you with my auto-da-fé. I shall not touch your body, I shall not confiscate your assets, I shall not violate your political rights. You will even be permitted to vote. But you will never be able to be voted, elected. Nor followed, nor respected. Because using my laws on freedom of opinion I shall say that you are impure. A wretch, a lunatic, a liar, a dissolute, a sinner. And I shall condemn you to civil death. I shall make you a criminal, a culprit, an outlaw and people will not listen to you any longer. More than that: not to be punished in their turn, those who think like you will abandon you». Then he adds that in the inanimate democracies, in the inertly democratic regimes, everything can be stated except the truth. Everything can be expressed, everything can be spread, except the freedom of revealing the truth. Because the truth leaves no way out, and inspires fear. Most people give in to fear and, out of fear, draw an insuperable line around the freedom which reveals the truth. An invisible but insurmountable barrier behind which one can only keep silent or join the chorus. If the impure one crosses that line, if he or she jumps that barrier, punishment descends on him or her at the speed of light. Worse: to make this possible are precisely those who secretly think as he or she does, but who out of prudence do not raise their voice against the anathemas and the excommunications. In fact, for a while, they beat behind the bush. They trifle, they keep the foot in both camps. But soon they fall silent and, terrified by the risk that such ambiguity exposes to, they sneak away. They abandon the criminal, the culprit, the outlaw to his or her fate. Basically what the Apostles do when they abandon Christ who has been arrested by order of the Sanhedrin and, after Caipha's roguery, leave him alone. That is, on the Way of the Cross.

Let's clear this up, then. Nor the one nor the other punishment worries me. The death of the body because, the more I hate death and I see in it a waste of the nature, the less I fear it. (Both in peace and in war, in health and in sickness, with death I have always played. So anyone who thinks to frighten me with the spectre of the cemetery makes a big blunder). The death of the soul because I'm used to be considered an outlaw and, the more they try to gag me or anathematize me or to excommunicate me, the more I disobey. The

stronger I get. (This recidivous heresy proves it).
What does worry me, therefore, is the insuperable line that most of the Westerners have drawn
around Thought. The insurmountable barrier
behind which you can only keep silent or join the
chorus of the condemnations, the concert of lies
which express reverence for the enemy and lack
of respect for those who fight him. Always. I will
give you an example which at first glance might
seem insignificant, frivolous, but which I find
very emblematic and disquieting.

When in October 2002 I published in Italy
the text of the lecture I had given at the American
Enterprise Institute in Washington, (title «Wake
up, West, wake up»), I hoped that a debate would
arise around it. My Wake up-West mainly spoke
of the sleep which has narcotized Europe and
transformed it into Eurabia, thus it deserved a debate. But instead of an invitation to think, to wake
up and think, the «pacifists» saw in it a warmonge-
ring formula. A racist, xenophobic, reactionary
slogan, a blasphemy. All of them. All. Even those
of the gayesque ultracapitalist world which manu-
factures billion-dollar rags. I mean the futile, silly,
trivial milieu of the so-called Haute Couture. And
a few months later a famous Roman fashion-house presented a collection which according to its
unlearned stylist was inspired by «Peace and

Unity among Peoples». (Sic). To be exact, on twelve heroines of History. Twelve saintly women who had-made-a-crucial-contribution-to-the-triumph-of-pacifism. Joan of Arc, to begin with, who wielded a sword better than Genghis Khan and commanded an army. Isabella of Castile, to go on, who had kicked out the Moors and ruthlessly exterminated a lot of them. Mary Queen of Scots who used to cut the head off anybody who opposed the Counter-Reformation. Catherine the Great of Russia who was notoriously a tyrant and had ascended the throne assassinating her husband. Marie Antoinette who cared about people as much as I care for the soccer game. And others along the same lines. (In fact only two of them were not questionable in that sense: Marilyn Monroe who as a pacifist had never distinguished herself for a particular exploit or struggle, however, and Bernadette whose only merit has been in my opinion the one of having brought the tourism to Lourdes). But the point is not the obscene ignorance which marked that selection. The point is that, to counterbalance the twelve saints, there was a thirteenth woman. A perfidious and ignoble creature, an instigator of war and discord, a witch, whose identity the fashion-house kept shrouded in the utmost mystery. Finally, though, the shroud of mystery vanished. Because the perfidious and

249

ignoble creature, the instigator of war and discord, the witch, appeared on the catwalk. And guess who she was. It was me, impersonated by a swaggering blonde with black glasses and black man's hat and black (leather) trousers and a T-shirt bearing the exhortation «Wake up, West». Over the T-shirt, an army-jacket literally lined with bullets. The 12.7 millimetre bullets that usually load the machine-guns. And that the swaggering blonde displayed with smiling complacency.

The insuperable line, the insurmountable barrier, prevails in America too. I know. (Not by chance Tocqueville identified the phenomenon studying democracy in America not in Europe where, at his times, real democracy did not exist as yet. And this includes also post-revolutionary France plus Great Britain). And, to assert that it prevails in America too, here I choose the striking example provided by the beautiful monument which stood before the State Judicial Building of Birmingham, Alabama. A granite plinth with a great marble open book. On the two exposed pages, the Ten Commandments: the genesis of our moral principles. As I'm told, the people of Birmingham were proud of that great marble book. And so was the State Governor: an impartial white man, a man much beloved also by the blacks who in Birmingham are almost always Christians.

Baptists, Methodists, Presbyterians, Lutherans, Catholics. But one ugly day the representatives of the tiny Muslim minority began muttering that the Ten Commandments had been written by the Jew Moses, that showing them in public clearly favoured Judaic-Christian culture, and the Politically Correct brigade sided with Allah. The protest ended up in the Supreme Court, the Solomons of the Supreme Court decided that in addition to harming Interreligious Dialogue the marble book violated the principles underpinning the separation of the Church from the State, and another ugly day the beautiful monument was removed in defiance of the State Governor who refused to accept the verdict and resigned. As for the other examples, look: they are so many that it would take an encyclopaedia to list them all. Take the fascistic radicals who, like their European colleagues, want to abolish Christmas. With Christmas, the giant fir-tree erected every year at the Rockefeller Center in New York. Take the half-witted and pretentious and ultra billionaires Hollywood stars who live as Sybarites but play the comedy of the Third-Worldism. Take the opportunists and presumed teachers who infest the universities and tell their students that western culture is an inferior or a pernicious culture. (While I translate this page, two years later, I think of the bandmaster who bears the last name of Churchill. Who dishonours it by teaching Ethics at the University of Colorado where he teaches Ethics, and who says that the World Trade Center Towers were a «legitimate target». That September 11 attack was «a natural and unavoidable consequence of the unlawful US policy, of its global financial empire, of the genocide perpetrated with the sanctions in Iraq». Then he adds that the three thousand five hundred dead were «a technocratic Nazi corps like the good Germans of Nazi Germany». Closing argument: «Sort-of-civilians? Innocent-people? Give me a break!»). However in America those who express contempt for the Nazi trash like the trash who dishonour Churchill name are not pilloried and derided and put under trial. They are not depicted as war-mongers with the jacket lined by bullets. In Europe-Eurabia, instead, they are martyrized how Tocqueville wrote almost two centuries ago. Thus, before drawing my conclusions, I want to say what there is behind this misdeed.

*   *   *

There is, above all, the decline of intelligence. Individual intelligence and collective intelligence. I mean the unconscious intelligence which guides the survival instinct and the conscious intelligence which guides the capability of understanding, of learning, of judging, and therefore of distinguishing the Good from the Evil. That's right. Paradoxically we are less intelligent than we were when we couldn't fly and go to Mars, when we could not replace a severed arm or a lost eye or a diseased heart, when we could not clone a sheep or ourselves. We are less lucid, less awake, than we were when we didn't have schools accessible to everybody, informations available to everybody, technologies which removing the torment of hunger and the fear of tomorrow make life easier for everybody. When this cornucopia did not exist, we had to solve things all by ourselves. Thus we had to force ourselves to rationalize, to think with our own heads. Not today. Because even in the small daily things our current society provides already-taken decisions, already-taken solutions. Solutions wrapped up like pre-cooked food. «We are thinking for you. So you don't have to» says a chilling caption that flashes up in a corner of the TV screen when I select the «Science and Science-Fiction» channel. (Which is more or less what the damn computers do when they correct presumed mistakes or offer suggestions that exonerate people from the duty of knowing the proper spelling. And that relieving us from responsibility lead us to obtuseness).

Ergo, people don't think anymore. Or they think without thinking with their own heads. Even to make an addition or a subtraction or a multiplication or a division. When I was a child, everybody could make an addition, a subtraction, a multiplication, a division. Even the illiterates. In grocery stores there were steelyards giving weights not prices. So the shop-keeper had to use his brain to work out the price of a cheese bit that weighed one hundred and twenty-five grams, of a fish that weighed six hundred and thirty-nine grams, of a chicken that weighed one kilo and two hundred seventy grams. Which he did. Rapidly, perfectly. In fact, if you were stupid, you couldn't run a greengrocer's or fishmonger's or a butcher's shop. Today anybody can. Even the illiterate who besides lining me with bullets do not know who Joan of Arc or Mary Queen of Scots or Marie Antoinette or Catherine the Great were. Because, instead of the steelyard, they have electronic scales which think for them. And which along with the weight give the price. Besides, when I was a child, gas cookers and electric cookers were owned by the rich only. To cook an egg you had to use coal and light the fire. You also had to keep the coal ignited with bellows. Not today. Today you turn a knob and the electric or gas cooker self-ignites. A big advantage if you use the spared time to think, to rationalize, to engage your mind in the

254

sphere of ideas, to understand that something in what you see or hear is wrong and hides a deception. An imposture. But you don't. Because...

Because the brain is like a muscle. And as any other muscle it needs to be exercised. If it is not exercised, it becomes lazy. Sluggish. It atrophies like my legs when I sit at this desk for months, for months I don't walk. And, while atrophying, the brain becomes less intelligent. Worse: it becomes stupid. Becoming stupid it loses the ability of reasoning, of judging, and delivers itself to the others' already-taken decisions. To the others' already-taken solutions. It surrenders to thoughts already processed and wrapped like pre-cooked food. Recipes, by the way, rather than thoughts. Indoctrination's formulas, rather than ideas. The formula of pacifism. The formula of imperialism. The formula of pietism. The formula of goody-goodism. The formula of racism. The formula or rather the recipe of conformism, of cowardice. Without realizing it, of course. Know why? Because those formulas or recipes are colourless, tasteless, odourless poisons. A kind of arsenic taken for too long. And nothing is more defenceless, therefore more malleable and manipulable, than an atrophied brain. Than a stupid brain. A brain which doesn't think or thinks with other people's brains. As a consequence, you can stuff it with anything you want:

from the fable of Allah's mercy to the dogma of Mary's virginity. You can make it believe that Jesus was a prophet of Islam, that he had nine wives and eighteen concubines, that he preached an eye for an eye and a tooth for a tooth, that he died of pneumonia when he was eighty-five. You can convince it that Socrates was a Syrian from Damascus, Plato an Iraqi from Baghdad, Copernicus an Egyptian from Cairo, Leonardo da Vinci a Moroccan from Rabat and that all the four of them studied at the University of Kabul. You can persuade it that Bush is Hitler's heir and reads *Mein Kampf* every morning at breakfast. That Sharon is so fat because he eats Palestinian children, that Islamic culture is a superior culture, that without Islam the West would not exist. You can make it believe that multi-culturalism is the Categorical Imperative extolled by Immanuel Kant, that our salvation is in the Koran, that the Muslims want to integrate, that the rainbow flags are the symbol of peace. And that people like me are reactionaries, war-mongers, assassins. No longer capable of thinking with its own head, not even capable of lighting a fire, of understanding that two plus two makes four, that atrophied brain will accept any lie or nonsense. It will store it up and spit it back out as automatically as we turn the gas knob or read off the price of a chicken from an electronic scale. Just atrophied? I should say lobotomized. Lobotomy is a mental castration very similar to the sexual castration. It consists in severing the nerve pathways which control cerebral processes like the testicular cords control the testicles. When you get a lobotomy you stop thinking. When you get a castration you stop having sexual desires. In both cases you become a docile instrument in the hands of your mutilator. And, if this one thinks what he thinks out of fear, (usually he does), along with the recipes or formulas he will transmit his fear to the lobotomized one. The decline of intelligence, in fact, always has a natural companion: fear.

* * *

Let me quote it again, this word that I abhor and that however I use to the point of monotony: the word «fear». Fear of thinking and, in thinking, of reaching conclusions which do not match those of the formulas imposed by the others. Fear of speaking and, in speaking, of reaching a judgement which is different from the judgement accepted by most. Fear of not being sufficiently aligned, obedient, servile, and therefore of being condemned to the civil death with which inert or rather inanimate democracies blackmail the citizens.

Fear of being free, in short. Of taking risks, of having courage. «The secret of happiness is freedom, and the secret of freedom is courage» said Pericles who knew what he was talking about. But today happiness is pursued through less noble means, and courage is a luxury. An extravagance which is derided or considered madness. Cowardice, on the contrary, is a food on sale for a few pennies and in any shop. The shop of the bullies who sell it rolled up in the paper of false revolutions. The shop of the impostors who play the valiant only when they risk nothing. The shop of the nullities who live on the ambiguities and the misinterpretations of equality. Those who have no courage always recur to equality. Never to freedom. Indeed Tocqueville was right when he said that the marriage on which democracy is based, the marriage between Equality and Freedom, has not succeeded. And it has not succeeded because we can be equal also in slavery. Because human beings love freedom much less than equality. And they love it much less because, flowing into collectivism, equality relieves the individual from the burden of responsibility. Because equality does not demand the sacrifice that freedom demands, does not require the courage that freedom requires. In short, it does not need freedom. Indeed Tocqueville is right also when he says that in democracy the term Equality means the legal equality expressed by the motto «All men are equal before the Law». Not a mental and moral equality. Not an equality of value and intelligence and guts. Finally, he is right when he says that in democracy votes are counted not weighed. Which is the reason why, in democracy, quantity ends up with being more valuable than quality. And why the unintelligent or the less intelligent always end up with ruling the others.

Well, Tocqueville said also that we should not be too hard on our fellows who make mistakes. But about this I do not agree. «A compassionate doctor cures no illness» my mother used to say when as a child I didn't want her to disinfect a wound with neat alcohol. And it is not with keeping silent or singing undeserved praises that we invite people to search their conscience, to extinguish the fire of Troy. Thus let me conclude with the hardest question I ever asked myself: is it still possible to extinguish that fire, that arson? Have we already lost, in the West, or not?

* * *

Perhaps not. I say so having in my mind's eyes the glorious show that 2004 New Year's Eve the city of New York offered the world in Times

Square. Many were afraid of a nuclear attack, that New Year's Eve in New York. The danger that the Defence Department indicates with the colour green when it is low, blue when it is considerable, yellow when it is serious, orange when it is very serious, red when it is mortal, was on orange. And the city had never lived in such an alarm. National Guard troops sent from all over the State in battledress, thousands of police officers positioned to protect locations like tunnels, bridges, underpasses, ports, airports. Helicopters and Air Force planes incessantly crossing the sky. Teams of scientists and doctors ready to measure possible radiation and try to neutralize it. As well as television news broadcasts advising the people at home to keep the windows shut and the medicine-chest handy. And, of course, the presumed nuclear attack did not exclude the nightmare of massacres carried out by the traditional method that is with explosives. In fact three targets were seen at maximum risk: the Statue of Liberty, the Brooklyn Bridge, and Times Square. The square where every New Year's Eve people gather en masse. Not at random my friend Tony D'Angelo, a city detective, had warned me: «On the evening of December 31 stay away from Times Square. Should something happen, it would be a bloodbath worse than September 11». And to reassure him I had told him that I detest being in crowds, that crowds give me claustrophobia. Thus for New Year's Eve I never go to Times Square, I watch the show on TV.

I watched it. And, when I switched TV on, I didn't expect to see many people. Not only because the danger was really significant but because during the week I had observed the arrangements and, rather than a location to host a joyful feast, Times Square had seemed to me an immense open-air prison. Checkpoints, watchtowers, metal-detector arches. Roadblocks, crash barriers to mark off the enclosures where the party-goers would check one-by-one and would be confined, corridors for the troops and for the police on foot or horseback... In that sense only tanks with cannons were missing, and for heaven's sake: who wants to celebrate New Year's Eve in an open-air prison? Yet no less than a million people stayed there. The square wasn't enough to hold the crowd, and for at least one mile this overflew into the adjacent thoroughfares. To make the individual checks easier, many had arrived in the afternoon, and had been standing in the cold for hours. But the finest thing wasn't even that. It was the joyfulness, at the same time unrestrained and calculated, which electrified them. The provocative insolence with which everybody reacted to the risk of another September 11. In fact everybody was wearing a comical orange cap provided by the City Hall. Each cap consisting in a sausage-shaped balloon of orange colour, the colour of the very-serious-risk. Each person, singing the refrain of the well-known song "New York, New York". Some in the original version: «New York is a wonderful town». Others, in an improvised version: «New York is a courageous town». The only one who did not sing was mayor Bloomberg who upright on the stage and pale with tension stared at the tops of the skyscrapers where the sharpshooters were aiming their telescopic-sight rifles or scanning the enclosures with doctors and technicians keeping the radiation-reading equipment. The best, however, took place at midnight. Because at midnight, while the fireworks split the blackness and everyone burst into a roar, TV cameras zoomed on a young man kneeling down at a girl's feet. A guy who in his right hand held a ring, in his left hand a placard on which it was written in big letters: «Will you marry me?». And the girl looked astonished, almost petrified, by disbelief. But suddenly she bent on him, she kissed him greedily. He turned the placard, and on its back the placard wore these words: «I knew she would say yes». So the crowd went wild. Some jumping up and down, some hugging each other, some chanting Hallelujah-Hallelujah, some yelling: «Many children, many children!». As if September 11 had never happened. And I was moved. Because it was a real defiance, that «many children». It truly meant: «We have no fear». And because not far away there was the enormous void left by the Twin Towers. There were the three thousand dead reduced to dust. The dead of September 11.

Yes, I was moved. I who never shed tears. And I set aside the ugly story of the Ten Commandments dislodged by the Constitutional Court in Birmingham, Alabama. I set aside the anger I feed for the half-witted who want to remove the Christmas Tree from the Rockefeller Center. I set aside the contempt I feel for the multimillionaire third-worlder Hollywood stars, the bastards dressed up as University professors, the wretches who support pro-Islamic obscenities of pro-Islamic UN. I set aside the disappointments that America has inflicted and inflicts upon me and upon Americans who fight like me, and I savoured the salt of hope. The same hope I feel when I look at the photos transmitted by the probes seeking life on Mars, while looking at them I think: we cannot lose. We cannot because Islam is a pond. And a pond is a cavity full of stagnant water. Water that never moves, never runs, never purifies itself, never becomes clean, never flows toward the sea and reaches the sea. In fact the pond pollutes easily, and even as a watering pool for cattle is worthless. It poisons, it kills. The pond does not love Life. It loves Death. Which is why kamikazes' mothers celebrate their sons' death and happily shout Allah-akbar, God is great, when their sons disintegrate with their victims. The West, instead, is a river. My home is a river. And rivers are courses of living water. Water that runs, that flows, and in flowing it purifies itself, renews itself. Water that collects other water, reaches the sea, and never mind if at times it floods. Never mind if at times its vitality overthrows even the dykes. The river loves Life all the same. It loves Life with all the good and the evil that it contains. Which is why our mothers weep when their children die. And why we seek Life everywhere. Why we find it even in the deserts, even in the steppes, even beyond the stratosphere, even on the Moon, even on Mars. And if we don't find it we bring it. Somehow we fabricate it, we fix the problem.

No, we cannot lose. And while I say so I realize that such faith of mine does not come from the photos taken by the probes sent to Mars. It does not come from our capability of going into the cosmos, of seeking Life on other planets. It comes from what I saw on New Year's Eve. From the joyful orange caps, the insolent orange balloons, the young man who despite the risk of another September 11 asked the girl to marry him. From the girl who said yes, from the crowd that yelled Hallelujah, many-children, Hallelujah. And this is the point.

* * *

It is because I saw all that in New York's Times Square, not in London's Trafalgar Square or in Paris' Place de la Concorde or in Madrid's Plaza Mayor or in Berlin's Alexanderplatz or in Moscow's Red Square. Even less, in Rome's Piazza San Pietro or in Venice's Piazza San Marco or in Florence's Piazza della Signoria or in Milano's Piazza della Scala. And to put out the fire of Troy, America alone is not enough. America is strong, yes. It's generous. So strong and generous that in the last sixty years it has already put out a couple of fires of calamities. The calamity of Nazi-Fascism and the calamity of Communism. But those were fires which could be put out with armies. With artillery, tanks, bombs. This one cannot. Despite the massacres with which the sons of Allah have been bloodying us and themselves over thirty years, in fact, the war that Islam has declared on the West is not really a military war. It's a cultural war. A war, Tocqueville would say, that instead of our body wants to strike our soul. Our way of life, our philosophy of Life. Our way of thinking, of acting, of loving. Our freedom.

Don't be fooled by their explosives. They are just a strategy. Those death's lovers don't kill us just for the pleasure of killing: they kill us to break our spirit. To intimidate us, to discourage us, to blackmail us. Their aim is not to simply fill our cemeteries, to simply destroy our skyscrapers. Our Eiffel Towers, our Towers of Pisa, our cathedrals, our Michelangelo's Davids. Their aim is to destroy our souls, our ideas, our achievements, our dreams. Meaning, to subjugate once more the West. And the real face of the West is not America. It is Europe. Though being Europe's child, Europe's inheritor, America does not have Europe's cultural physiognomy. Europe's cultural past, Europe's cultural features, Europe's cultural identity. Though being the other face of the West, America is not the West that Islam wants to subjugate. The West in which Süleyman the Magnificent wanted to establish the «Islamic State of Europe». His appendix of Ottoman Empire. An appendix geographically close to that empire, by the way. Not so far as the continent just discovered beyond the Atlantic Ocean, I mean the continent that would be called America. Today's Troy burns in Europe, not in America. Thus to extinguish that fire it takes, first of all and above all, Europe. But how to count on a Europe which has become Eurabia, which welcomes and favours the enemy, which even grants him the vote?!? How to trust a Europe which to that enemy sells itself like a whore, a Europe which is no longer capable of reasoning?

The decline of intelligence is the decline of Reason. And everything which now happens in Europe, in Eurabia, is also a decline of Reason. A decline which before being morally wrong is intellectually wrong. Refusing to admit that all Islam is a pond inside which we are drowning, in fact, is against Reason. Not defending our territory, our homes, our children, our dignity, our essence, is against Reason. Accepting the silly or cynical lies which are dispensed to us like arsenic inside the soup is against Reason. Resigning ourselves, surrendering out of cowardice or sloth is against Reason. Dying of thirst and solitude in a desert which denies the Future is against Reason. Also thinking that the Fire of Troy might extinguish by itself or by a miracle of the Madonna is against Reason. So listen to me, I beg you. Listen to me because, as I've said many times, I do not write for fun or for

267

money. I write out of duty. A duty which is costing my life. And out of duty I have pondered a lot on this tragedy. In the last four years I've done nothing else but anatomizing Islam and the West, analyzing their crimes and our fouls. That is, fighting the war we can no longer avoid or ignore. To do so, I have even put aside the novel I was writing, the book I called «my baby». Worse: I have even ignored myself, my survival. At such a point that now I haven't much to live. And I would like to die thinking that such sacrifice has been of some use. That I haven't done like the parent who wears himself out in the effort of explaining his son what is Good and what is Evil, but instead of listening the son counts the ants which pass by then yawns: «One hundred! There are one hundred!». In my lecture «Wake up, West, wake up» I said that the West has lost passion. That we must regain passion, the force of passion. And God knows if this is true. Living takes passion. Refusing to submit, to comply, to surrender, means living with passion. But Europe does not refuse at all to submit, to comply, to surrender. On the contrary, it cowardly waves a white flag of servitude and resignation which is suicide itself. The fact is that, at the point we have reached, it isn't only a matter of living: it is a matter of surviving. And, more than passion, surviving needs reason. Ratiocination, reason. So this time I do not appeal to rage, to pride. I do not even appeal to passion. I appeal to Reason. And together with Mastro Cecco, once more condemned to death by irrationality, suicidal insanity, I say: we need to rediscover the Force of Reason.

Oriana Fallaci

Florence, June 2003
New York, April 2004

POST-SCRIPT

(Four years after September 11)

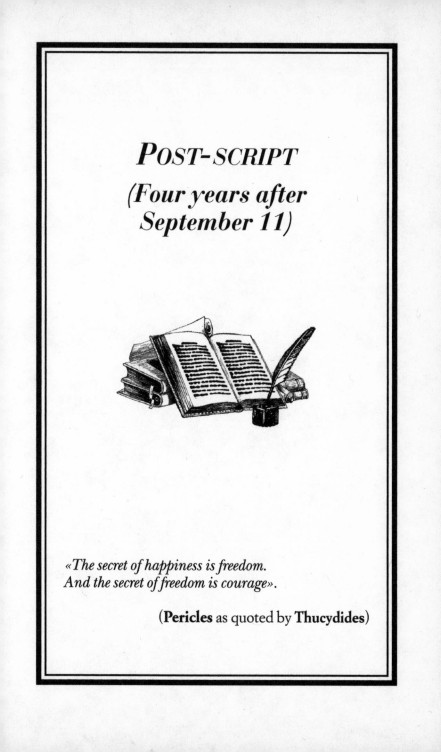

*«The secret of happiness is freedom.
And the secret of freedom is courage».*

(**Pericles** as quoted by **Thucydides**)

PUBLISHERS' NOTE

This is the speech that Oriana Fallaci delivered on November 28th 2005 when the Center for the Study of Popular Culture conferred to her the «Annie Taylor award» «to honour her heroism and valor as a symbol of the Resistance to Islamo-fascism and as a warrior in the cause of human freedom».

The award was presented in New York by Daniel Pipes author and founder of the Middle East Forum Campus Watch, by David Horowitz author and founder of the Center for the Study of Popular Culture as well as editor of «Front Page Magazine», by Robert Spencer author and director of the Jihad Watch. All three, scholars of Islam and Islam history. «The Annie Taylor award» said the motivation «is given to individuals who have shown exceptional courage against great odds and in the face of great danger. Today there are few people alive who deserve it as much as Oriana Fallaci».

Given its topic, a topic which besides expressing her strong link with the United States accentuates her unshakable independence of thought, we asked Oriana Fallaci to publish the speech as a post-script to the text of «The Force of Reason». And, also considering that often it refers to concepts and facts cointained in «The Force of Reason», she agreed. «All right» she said. «This will demonstrate that my ideas and my struggle against the nazi-fascism of Islam revival have not changed. As a matter of fact, they have reinforced and will reinforce until I'll have a breath of life».

The Publishers

JUMPING OVER
NIAGARA FALLS

Well! An award inspired by a woman who jumped over Niagara Falls (and survived) is a thousand times more precious and prestigious and above all more ethical than an Oscar or a Nobel Prize, until yesterday glorious bestowals conferred to people of value and today disrespected gratuities given to the Islamophile and Westphobic and anti-American devotees. To the Islam's lackeys who impudently acting as enlightened gurus define Bush as an assassin, Sharon as a war-criminal, Castro as a philanthropist, the United States as «the most ferocious and barbarous and ghastly power ever existed in history». In fact, should I find myself awarded by one of those two disrespected gratuities, (thank God a probability as far as the farthest Black Hole in the Universe), I would sue the jury for defamation and slander. On the contrary, I accept this «Annie Taylor» with gratitude and pride. And who cares if it overestimates my guts.

Yes: especially as a war correspondent, during my life I have made several jumps. In Vietnam for instance, I've often jumped into trenches to avoid mortar fire and other mishaps. As often, from US helicopters to reach the combat-fields. In Bangladesh, even from a Russian one to join from Calcutta the battle of Dacca. While interviewing the rascals of the world, the Khomeinis and the Arafats and the Gaddafis etcetera, I've also jumped into quixotic quarrels which put my existence in serious jeopardy. And once, in Latin America, I've jumped from a high window to escape local police's arrest. But never, never, have I jumped over Niagara Falls. And I never would. Too hazardous, too dangerous. More dangerous than writing the Truth. More hazardous than having independence of thought, than being a dissident (meaning an outlaw) in a society which sells to the enemy its homeland, its culture, its civilization, its dignity. Thus thank you, Daniel Pipes, David Horowitz, Robert Spencer. And please believe me when I say that this award is yours as well as mine. That you are my comrades-in-arms, my pals, my buddies. That you fight this war as much as I do. In fact when I was told that this year you had chosen to award *la* Fallaci, I asked myself: «Shouldn't I be the one who awards them?». And in order to reciprocate the tribute, I fancied to present you some kind of medal or trophy. Tonight I came empty hands only because I didn't know, I wouldn't know, where to buy that stuff. You see: with medals and trophies I have an exiguous, really exiguous, familiarity. Here is why.

To begin with, we seem to live in real democracies, in sincere and vivacious democracies ruled by freedom of thought and opinion, whereas we live in idle and weak democracies ruled by despotism and fear. As I write in *The Force of Reason*, fear of thinking and in thinking of reaching conclusions which don't match those of the Islam's lackeys in command. Fear of speaking and, in speaking, of reaching a judgment different from the judgment slyly imposed by them. Fear of not being sufficiently aligned, obedient, servile, and therefore banned through the moral exile with which idle and weak democracies blackmail the citizen. Fear of being free, in short, of taking risks, of having courage. «The secret of happiness is freedom, and the secret of freedom is courage» said Pericles who knew what he was talking about. Again I take this statement from that book and from it I also take the explanation that almost two hundred years ago Alexis de Tocqueville gave with his undying milestone *Democracy in America*. Sorry to repeat myself. But in order to be heard by the deaf, or supposed deaf, repeating is never enough.

In dictatorial or absolutist regimes, Tocqueville writes, despotism strikes the body. It does so by putting the body in chains, by torturing or suppressing it in various ways. Beheadings, hangings, shootings, stonings, Inquisition's burnings etcetera. And in doing so it ignores the soul which can rise intact over the mangled flesh, make a hero out of a victim. In the inanimate democracies, in the inertly democratic regimes, on the contrary, despotism ignores the body and attacks the soul. Because it is the soul that despotism wants to put in chains. To torture, to suppress. Thus, its victims are never told as they are in dictatorial or absolutist regimes: «Either you think as I do, either you die». They are told: «Choose. You are free not to think or to think as I do. If you don't think as I do, I shall not suppress you with my autos-da-fé. I shall not touch your body, I shall not confiscate your assets, I shall not violate your political rights. You will be even permitted to vote. But you will never be elected. You'll be never followed and respected. Because, using my laws on freedom of thought and opinion, I shall say that you are impure. A liar, a dissolute, a sinner, a wretch, a lunatic. I shall make you an outlaw, a criminal, I shall condemn you to Civil Death. And people will not listen to you any longer. More than that: not to be punished in their turn, those who think like you will desert you».

This happens, he explains, thanks to the fact that in the inanimate democracies, in the inert democratic regimes, everything can be stated except the Truth. Everything can be spread except the thinking which reveals the Truth. Because the Truth inspires fear. Because in reading or hearing the Truth most people surrender to fear and out of fear they draw a no-trespassing line around it. They built an invisible but insurmountable barrier inside which one can only keep silent or join the chorus. If the dissident crosses that line, if he or she jumps over the Niagara Falls of that barrier, punishment descends on him or on her at the speed of light. And those who make it possible are precisely the people who secretly think as he or she does but who out of convenience or cowardice don't raise their voices against the anathemas and the persecutions. The friends, very often. Or the so-called friends. The partners. Or the so-called partners. The colleagues. Or the so-called colleagues. In fact, for a while, they beat behind the bush. They trifle, they keep a foot in both camps. But soon they become silent and, terrified by the risks that such ambiguity exposes to, they sneak away. They abandon the outlaw to his or her fate, and with their silence they give their approval to his or to her Civil Death. (Something that I have experienced all over my life but especially in these last years. «I can support you no longer» said to me, two or three Christmas ago, a famous Italian journalist who had written two editorials in my defense. «Why?» I sadly asked. «Because people don't talk to me anymore, don't invite me at dinner anymore» he replied).

The other why concerning my exiguous familiarity with medals and trophies stays in the fact that, since September 11, the most of Europe has become a Niagara Falls of McCarthyism substantially identical to the one which afflicted this country half a century ago. The only difference, its political colour. Because half a century ago it was the Left which was victimized by McCarthyism. Today it is the Left which victimizes all the others with McCarthyism. Its McCarthyism. In Europe much more than in the United States. From any point of view, today's Europe overflows with a Witch Hunt that hits anyone going against the stream. It does so with a new Inquisition which sets fire to the heretics by muzzling or trying to muzzle them. Because yes: we too abound with Torquemadas like your Ward Churchills, your Noam Chomskys, your Louis Farrakhans, your Michael Moores of the Caviar Left. We too are infected by a plague against which all antidotes seem to fail. The plague of a combined new nazi-fascism: the Islamic nazism and the autochthonous fascism. Its first germ-carriers, the presumed educators who more and more scatter the infection even in the elementary schools and pre-schools where exposing a Baby Jesus' crib or a Santa Claus with toys is considered an «insult to Muslim children»; who more and more intensify that infection in the High Schools and exasperate it in the universities. Its germs, the daily indoctrination exercised through the brainwashing. The Crusades' history rewritten thus falsified as in an Orwell's *1984*, for example. The slavish obsequiousness towards the Koran seen as a religion of peace and mercy, plus as a Beam of Light compared to which our civilization appears to be the spark of a cigarette butt. And along with that indoctrination, the political demonstrations. The ludicrous marches, the fascist assaults. This too, more and more. Do you know what the students of the radical Left did last October in the city of Turin, Italy? They assaulted the Renaissance church of Il Carmine and smeared the facade by spraying the words «Nazi-Ratzinger» (Pope Benedict XVI) then the admonition: «With the bowels of the priests we shall hang Pisanu». (Our Minister of the Interior Department). Then upon the facade they urinated: the same graciousness that Muslim hooligans like to perform on the cathedrals of my city, Florence. Finally they went inside the church and, scaring at death the poor old ladies who attended the Vespers' service, they blew up a petard next to the altar. All this, under the eyes of policemen who could not intervene. Guess why. Because in our leftist municipalities such misdeeds are considered freedom-of-expression. (Unless such a freedom takes place against the mosques, of course. But who dares touch a mosque?!?).

And no need to add that those youngsters' parents are no better. Do you know what happened last week at Marano, populous town located in the province of Naples? It happened that its mayor (an ex-seminarist, an ex-member of the deceased Italian Communist Party then of the still living Communist Refoundation Party, and now a member of the Party of the Italian Communists), cancelled tout-court the ordinance issued by the prefectorial commissioner to dedicate a street to the Martyrs of Nassiriyah. I mean to the nineteen Italian militaries who two years ago were blown up by kamikazes in Iraq. He cancelled it by asserting that the nineteen were not martyrs, they were mercenaries, and gave that street the name of Arafat. Yes, Arafat. He did so by placing a name-plate which says: «Yasser Arafat, the symbol of Palestinian Unity (sic) and Resistance». Then he flooded the other streets of Marano with posters saying the same thing and literally upholstered the City-Council Hall with gigantic photos of the aforesaid guy. The municipality building, with Palestinian flags.

The sordid and vile plague also propagates through newspapers, TV, Radio. Through a media which out of baseness or convenience or stupidity is in its overwhelming majority as Islamophile and as Westphobic and as anti-American as the presumed educators, the teachers. Which without any risk of being prosecuted more and more divulge fabrications that favour Islam. Without any worry of being scorned pass over in silence episodes similar to the Turin's or Marano's ones. More and more it also propagates through songs and guitars and rock concerts and movies, that plague. Through a show-business where, like your half-witted and pretentious and ultra-billionaire Hollywood court-jesters, our court-jesters play the role of goody-goodies always prompt to shed tears for the killers. (Never for the victims, of course). More and more it also propagates through a judiciary system which has lost any sense of justice, any knowledge of jurisdiction. I mean through the tribunals where, like your magistrates, our magistrates acquit terrorists as easily as they acquit pedophiles. And finally it scatters through the intimidation of good people in good faith. I mean the people who out of ignorance or fear endure such despotism and don't realize that their silence or submission helps the new combined nazi-fascism to grow. Not by chance, when I say these things, I really feel as a Cassandra who speaks to the wind. Or as one of the forgotten anti-fascists who seventy and eighty years ago warned the deaf and the blind from a couple called Mussolini and Hitler. But the deaf remained deaf, the blind remained blind, and both of them ended up with bearing on their foreheads what in *The Apocalypse* I call The Brand of Shame and Infamy.

As a consequence, since I wrote the Trilogy, (I mean *The Rage and the Pride*, *The Force of Reason*, and *Oriana Fallaci interviews herself* with the post-script I called *The Apocalypse*), my medals have been the insults. The denigrations and the abuses I receive from today's McCarthyism, today's Witch-Hunt, today's Inquisition. My trophies, the trials that in Europe I undergo for crime of opinion. A crime now disguised as «vilification of Islam, racism or religious racism, xenophobia, instigation to hate» etcetera. (Parenthesis: should Penal Code prosecute me for hate? Can hate be forbidden by Law? Hate is a sentiment. An emotion, a reaction, a feeling. Not a de-jure crime, a punishable offense. Like love, hate belongs to human nature. Better yet, to Life. It is the opposite of love and thus, like love, it cannot be forbidden by some article of some Penal Code. It can be judged, yes. It can be adversed, condemned. But only on a moral basis. For instance the moral basis of religions, which, like the Christian religion, preach love. Not on a legal basis. Not in a tribunal which grants me the right to love whom I want. Because, if I have the right to love whom I want, I also have and must have the right to hate whom I want. Starting from those who hate me. Yes, I do hate the Bin Ladens. I do hate the Zarkawis. I do hate the kamikazes and the beasts who cut off our heads and blow up our people and martyrize their women. I do hate the bastards who smear the facades of the churches and urinate on them. I do hate the Ward Churchills, the Noam Chomskys, the Louis Farrakhans, the Michael Moores, their accomplices, and the domestic traitors who sell us to the enemy. I do hate them as much as I hated Mussolini and Hitler and Stalin and Company. I do hate them as I always hated any murder of Freedom. It is my sacrosanct right. My sacrosanct duty. And if I am wrong, tell me why those who hate me even more than I hate them are not prosecuted with the same indictment. Tell me why this instigation-to-hate's matter never touches the professional haters. I mean the new McCarthyists who persecute me with their strategy of civil death and the Muslims who on the concept of hate have built their ideology. Their philosophy. Parenthesis closed).

They take place in whatsoever country a son of Allah or a traitor of ours wants to silence me through the Penal Code, those trials. They take place in Paris, France. La France Eternelle, la Patrie du Laicisme, la Bonne Mère du Liberté-Egalité-Fraternité, where for vilification-of-Islam only my friend Brigitte Bardot has gone through more ordeals than I have. La France Liberale, Progressiste, where as I tell in the second book of the Trilogy three years ago the French Jews of «Licra» (the Jewish leftist association that likes to manifest raising photos of Ariel Sharon with a swastika on his brow-ridge) and the French Muslim of «Mrap» (the Islamic leftist association that likes to manifest raising posters of Bush with swastikas on his eyes) wanted to lock me in jail and confiscate *La Rage et l'Orgueil*. Or to sell it with such warning on the jacket: «Attention! This book may be a danger to your mental health». (Together they also wanted to pocket a huge pecuniary penalty, of course). They take place in Berne, Switzerland. Die wunderschöne Schweiz, the wonderful Switzerland of Wilhelm Tell, where the Federal Secretary of Justice dared ask his Italian colleague to extradite me in handcuffs. Or in Bergamo, Northern Italy, where next trial will take place next June thanks to a judge who sounds very eager to grant me a few years of jail. (The penalty that for vilification-of-Islam is applied in my country. A country where with no legal consequence any Muslim can unhook a crucifix from the wall of a classroom or of a hospital then trow it in the garbage and say that the crucifix is rubbish portraying «a nude corpse invented to scare Muslim children»). And guess who promoted the Bergamo trial. One of the never-indicted, never-prosecuted, thus never convicted, crucifix-offenders. The author of a filthy booklet which is sold in every mosque, every islamic community, every leftist bookstore of Italy. And which under the title «Islam punishes Oriana Fallaci» urges the Prophet's disciples to eliminate me in observance of five Surahs regarding perverse women.

* * *

As for the threats to my life, for the sons of Allah's irresistible desire of slashing my troath or blowing me up or at least killing me with a gunshot, well: I shall limit myself to say that, especially when I am in Italy, I must be safeguarded twenty-four hours on twenty-four by the Carabinieri. Our military police. A protection which, though as necessary, as affectionate, is an unbearable limitation of my personal freedom. And as for the insults, the anathemas, the abuses that European media honours me with on behalf of the marriage Islam-Left, here are some of the qualifications I get. In quotes: «Abominable. Blasphemous. Deleterious.

Troglodyte. Racist. Retrograde. Ignoble. Wretched. Reactionary. Liar. Lunatic. Abject». Unquotes. As you see, words identical or very similar to those mentioned by Alexis de Tocqueville when he speaks of dictatorial or absolutist regimes, of inanimate democracies' despotism. In my country such despotism also delights in calling me «hyena», in distorting my name from Oriana to Or-Hyena, and in mocking me with Joan of Arc's sardonic identifications. «The bestialities of the neo-Joan of Arc». «Shut up, Joan of Arc». «That's enough, Joan of Arc». But there is something even worse. Because last August I was received in private audience by Ratzinger. I mean by Pope Benedict XVI. A Pope who loves my work since he read *Letter to a Child Never Born* and whom I deeply respect since I read his intelligent books. Moreover, with whom I happen to agree in many occasions. For example, when he writes that the West has developed a sort of hatred towards itself. That it no longer loves itself, that it has lost its spirituality and risks to lose its identity too. Exactly what I write when I write that the West is sick with a moral and intellectual cancer. In fact I often observe: «If a Pope and an atheist say the same thing, in that thing there must be something tremendously true».

New parenthesis: I am an atheist, yes. A Christian atheist, as I always point out, but an atheist.

And Pope Ratzinger knows it very well. In *The Force of Reason*, I dedicate a whole chapter to explaining the apparent paradox of such self-definition. Yet do you know what he says to atheists like me? He says: «Okay, (the okay is mine, of course), then Veluti si Deus daretur. Behave as if God existed». Words from which one assumes that in the religious community there are more open-minded and smarter people than in the secular one I belong to. So open-minded and so smart that they don't even try, not even dream, to save my soul. (I mean, to convert me). This is also why I state that, in selling itself to theocratic Islam, laicism (you say secularism) has missed the most important appointment offered to it by History. And in doing so it has opened a void, an abyss, that only spirituality can fill. It is also why in the Church of today I see an unexpected partner, an unexpected ally. In Ratzinger, and in any pious man who accepts my disquieting indipendence of thought and behaviour, a real compagnon-de-route. Unless, of course, the Church too misses its appointment with History. Something I don't foresee, though. And I don't because, in reaction to the materialistic ideologies which have characterized the century we just left, the century ahead seems to me marked by an inevitable nostalgia or irresistible need of religiousness. As much as religion, in fact, religiousness always ends up with being the simplest (if not the easiest) vehicle to reach spirituality. New parenthesis closed.

So we met, this smartly righteous gentleman and I. Free for ceremonials, formalities, all by ourselves in his study-room of Castel Gandolfo, we conversed for a while. And the non-professional encounter was supposed to stay secret. In my obsession for privacy, I had asked it to be so. But the rumour spread all the same. Like a nuclear bomb it reached the Italian press, and guess what a petulant idiot with academic requisites wrote in a most notorious and leftist newspaper of Rome: *La Repubblica*. He wrote that the Pope can see as much as he wants (in quotes) «people as trashy and impious and as sinful and as mentally ill» (unquotes) as Fallaci. Because (in quotes) «the Pope is not "una persona perbene", not a decent person». (Unquotes). Besides, and always thinking of Tocqueville's invisible no-trespassing line, I never forget what happened here in America four years ago. I mean when *The Rage and the Pride* article (not the book as yet) appeared in Italy, and the *New York Times* unchained its super-Political-Correctness with a full page correspondence from Rome which presented me as a «provocateur». As a villain guilty of slandering the noble Islam. When the book appeared in the United States, all the same. Because yes: the *New York Post* presented me as «the Conscience of Europe», as «the exception in a time where honesty and moral clarity are no longer considered precious virtues». Yes, in their letters its readers did generously define me as «the only eloquent intellect that Europe has produced since the day Winston Churchill had pronounced the famous *Step by Step* speech and warned Europe against Hitler». But the Caviar-Left newspapers and TV channels and radio stations kept mute as if their tongue had been cut by Zarkawi, or imitated *The New York Times*.

Even less I forget what has happened and happens in my country during this November 2005. Because, published by a company whose majority-shares is held by my Italian publishers, and by them flashily advertised on the daily paper I considered my professional family, the *Corriere della Sera*, another anti-Fallaci book has now reached the bookstores. A book written, this time, by a former vice-editor-in-chief of the ultracommunist daily which once belonged to the Italian Communist Party: *l'Unità*. I have not read it. I shall not read it. You see, at least six books have been written about me. (And still another one is about to appear in Italy very soon). Mostly, unauthorized biographies full of offensive lies and grotesque inventions. And I have never read one of them. Not even cast a glance on their covers. But I know that the title (of course accompanied by my name, a guarantee to sell for sure) contains the words «bad teacher». I know that the «bad teacher» is portrayed again as a sordid reactionary, a pernicious warmonger, a lethal carrier of «Orianism». And, according to the author, «Orianism» is a lethal virus. A contagious illness, a deadly disease, an impure obsession which kills people who get contaminated by it. (Thank God, several millions of people. In Italy only, the Trilogy has sold much more than four million copies in three years. And in other twenty European countries it's a solid bestseller).

Yet this is not all. Because, in the same days, the Center-Right mayor of Milano enclosed me in the list of the Little Ambroses: the much coveted golden medals that on the festivity of St. Ambrose the city grants to people-who-admirably-distinguish-themselves-in-our-society. And when my name was inserted in the list, the leftist voters unleashed a pandemonium which lasted until five in the morning. All over the night it was like witnessing a hen-house quarrel, I am told. Feathers flied all over, crests bleeded, cocodès' clucking deafened, and what a miracle that nobody ended in some Emergency Room. Then, the day after, they came back yelling that my Little Ambrose would pollute pluriculturalism and tarnish St. Ambrose's festivity. That it would give the prize-ceremony an anti-Islamic meaning, it would offend the Muslims and consequently the prize-winners of the Left. Those winners even threatened to refuse their awards and promised to stage a fierce demonstration against perverse Fallaci. The Communist Refoundation Party's leader also declared: «Giving that gold medal to Oriana Fallaci is like giving the Peace Nobel Prize to George W. Bush».*

* *Note of the Author*. A few weeks after the «Annie Taylor» and the «Little Ambrose», I was surprisingly awarded with one of the highest Italian bestowal: the golden medal that, on advice of the Ministry of Education, the President of the Republic confers to citizens who are judged most meritorious in the field of Culture. And, in order to pass under silence the very honourable recognition, the two major daily papers (starting with the one I considered my professional family) censored the news. Not only: around forty radical leftists (many professors of universities) addressed the President of the Republic with a perfidious letter accusing him to have awarded through me the intolerance, the racism, the xenophobia which sponsor the-clash-of-civilizations. Also, that in awarding me the President had committed an «act against the Italian Constitution». Soon after, an art-gallery of Milano opened an exhibit of paintings exalting Islam and anti-Americanism. To lead them, a big and macabre picture where, for the glory of Islam, I appear decapitated like the Americans executed with the halal-knife by the head-cutters of Iraq. From the severed neck, a gush of blood that spreads all over. And my eyes (very wicked eyes) wide open in terror.

This said, and just to render unto Caesar what belongs to Caesar, unto God what belongs to God, I must clear up something that may disappoint some or the most of you. And here it is. I am not a Conservative. I don't sympathize with the Right more than I do with the Left. Though I reject any political classification, I consider myself a revolutionary. Because in my view Revolution does not necessarily mean the Taking of the Bastille or the Taking of the Winter Palace. And certainly it does not mean guillotines, execution-squads, blood in the streets. In my view Revolution means to say «No» and struggle for that «No». Through that struggle, changing things. And for sure I say many «No». I always have. For sure there are many things that I would like to change. Thus, not to preserve. Not to conserve. One is the use and abuse of freedom not seen as Liberty but as licentiousness, capriciousness, viciousness, selfishness, irresponsibility, arrogance. Another one is the use and abuse of democracy not seen as the juridical marriage of equality and freedom but as a demagogic equalitarianism. A senseless denial of merit, a tyranny of the majority. (Alexis de Tocqueville, again). Still another, the lack of self-discipline. I mean the discipline without which the marriage of Equality and Freedom collapses. Still another, the nescience of honour and the triumph of pusillanimity in which we live and raise our children. All iniquities which characterize both the Right and the Left. My friends, if with its supercilious or bullish betrayals the Left has dishonoured and dishonours the good fights it fought in the past, with its ambiguities and pharisaisms the Right does not honour the role that it professes to have. Therefore, the terms Right and Left are for me two obsolete expressions to which I recur only out of habit or verbal convenience. And as I say in *The Force of Reason*, in both of them I see nothing but two football-teams which distinguish themselves only by the colour of their players' shirts. And which substantially play the same game: the game of catching the ball of Power. (Not the Power that rulers need to rule: the Power which exhausts itself in itself).

This may appear demagogic, oversimplified, even superficial: I know. But if you analyze the facts, you see that what I say is the bare truth. Beginning with the disaster which strikes us. For Christsake, nobody can deny that Europe's Islamic invasion has been backed and is backed by the Left. But nobody can deny either that such invasion would have never reached the level it has reached if the Right had not provided its complicity. If the Right had not given its imprimatur. Let's admit it: the Right has never moved a finger to stop or to hold back the growth of the Islamic invasion. An example? As in many other European countries, in Italy it is the leader of the official Right who supports the leftist impatience of granting the vote to immigrants without citizenship. This, in spite of the fact that our Constitution grants the vote to citizens only. Not to invaders or assassins or tourists.

As a result, I cannot be associated with the Right just as I cannot be associated with the Left. I cannot be an instrument of the Right just as I cannot be an instrument of the Left. And I am extremely if not equally annoyed with both of them. Whatever their location and nationality. At the present time, for instance, I am annoyed with the American Right which pushes the European leaders to accept Turkey as a member of the European Union. Exactly what the European Left has always worked for. But the victims of the Islamic invasion, the European citizens, do not want the Turkey in their home. People like me do not want Turkey at home. And Condolcezza Rice should stop exercising her realpolitik at our expenses. She is a smart woman, no doubt. For sure, smarter than most of her male and female colleagues both here in America and beyond the Atlantic. But about the country which for centuries was the Ottoman Empire, about the not-European Turkey, the Islamic-Turkey, she knows or pretends to know very little. And about the monstrous calamity that its entry in the European Union would represent, she knows or pretends to know even less. So I say: Ms. Rice, Mr. Bush, ladies and gentlemen of the American Right: if you believe so much in a country where women have spontaneously resumed the veil and where Human Rights are daily ridiculed, have it for yourselves. Ask the Congress to annex it to the United States as the Fifty-first State, and concentrate on Iran. Take care of its nuclear lasciviousness, of its obtuse and vicious hostages-kidnapper president, focus on its nazistic promise to wipe out Israel from the world's maps. Then you, Condolcezza, do something about it.*

* *Note of the Author*. «Con dolcezza» (two separate words) is one of the Italian terms employed by composers for indicating the interpretation that executors should give to a bar or to a phrase or to a page or to the whole score. It means «With sweetness». Ms. Rice doesn't use the name Condolcezza (one single word) she was given by her music-lover parents. She uses the mispelled version which was written by the not music-lover clerk who registered her birth at Birmingham, Alabama, municipality: Condoleeza. Thus, mine is not a typographical error. It is the liberty I take in never calling her Condoleeza. Despite her toughness, (thank God a toughness almost as tough as mine), I like to call her in the Italian way: Condolcezza. Withsweetness.

* * *

At the risk of disavowing the boundless respect that Americans claim towards any religion, I must also clear up what follows. (Besides, something that I already said in *The Force of Reason*). How come that, in a country where 85 percent of the citizens say to be Christian, so few rebel to the ludicrous offensive which is going on against Christmas?!? How come that so few protest when your Caviar Left speaks about abolishing Christmas-holidays, Christmas-trees, Christmas-songs, the same expressions Merry Christmas and Happy Christmas?!? How come that so few don't rebel against the phony liberals who like Talibans delight when in the name of secularism a Ten Commandment's monument gets removed from a Birmingham square? And how come that so many initiatives are taken, meanwhile, in favour of the Islamic religion? How come that in places like the Michigan suburb of Detroit, for instance, the predominantly Polish and Catholic Detroit where a Noise-Ordinance forbids the sound of the bells, Muslim minority has obtained that local muezzins broadcast their noisy prayers from 6 a.m. to 10 p.m.? How come that in a country where the Law orders to erase from public sites all symbols of Christianity and Christian prayers, companies like Dell Computers and Tyson Foods comply with the Islamic request of granting liturgical accomodations to their Islamic employers? And this in spite of the fact that their frequent prayers disrupt the assembly-line work? How come that professor Ward Churchill has not been fired by the University of Colorado for praising Bin Laden and September 11 but a Washington Radio host has been fired for accusing Muslim religion to be behind terrorism? Now, let me conclude this evening with the last crucial points.

First point. I do not see Islamic terrorism as the main weapon of the war that the sons of Allah have declared on us. Both in the Right and in the Left, everybody focuses on terrorism. Everybody. Even the leftist radicals. (Which does not surprise me because blaming terrorism is their alibi. Their way to clean their unclean conscience). But terrorism is only one face of this war. The most visibile, yes. The bloodiest and the most barbarous, of course. Yet, paradoxically, not the most pernicious. Not the most catastrophic. In my opinion, the most pernicious and most catastrophic is the religious one. The one from which all the other faces derive. Beginning with the face of immigration. Dear friends: it is immigration, not terrorism, the Trojan Horse which has penetrated the West and transformed Europe in Eurabia. It is immigration, not terrorism, the weapon for which since four years I cry «Troy burns-Troy burns». An immigration which in Europe-Eurabia far exceeds the Mexican trespass that (with the blessing of your Left and the imprimatur of your Right) the United States bear. Only in the twenty-five countries which form the European Union, at least twenty-five million Muslims. A number that does not include the illegal ones never expelled. Up to now, other fifteen million and probably more. And given the Muslim irrepressible inexorable implacable fertility, such figure is expected to double in 2016. To triple or to quadruple if Turkey becomes a European Union member. In fact Bernard Lewis prophesies that within 2100 the whole of Europe will be also numerically dominated by Muslims. And Bassam Tibi (the official deputy of the so-called Moderate Islam in Germany) adds: «The problem is not to establish whether within 2100 the greatest majority or the totality of Europeans will be Muslim: one way or another, they will. The problem is whether Islam destined to dominate Europe will be an Euro-Islam or the Islam of Sharia». Which is why I don't either believe in the Dialogue with Islam. Why I sustain that such dialogue is a monologue, a soliloquy nourished by our naïveté or unconfessed despair. And why, about this topic, I strongly dissent from Pope Ratzinger who insists on that monologue with dismaying hope. (Once again, Holy Father: of course I too would like a world where everybody loves everybody and nobody is enemy of anybody. But the enemy *is* there, Holy Father. It's there, and it has no intention of dialoguing with you and with us).

Second point. I don't either believe in the so-called pluri-culturalism's fib. (And, in connection with that fib: do you know that the Barbican Center Theater of London has censored *Tamburlaine the Great*, the drama written in 1587 by Christopher Marlowe? At a certain point of the drama, remember, Christopher Marlowe makes Tamburlaine burn the Koran. While the Koran burns, he also makes him challenge the Prophet by shouting: «Now, if you have the power, come down and make a miracle!». And, given the fact that these words and the Koran burning infuriated local Muslims, the Barbican Theater has cut off the whole scene). Even less I believe in the fib called Integration. Integration means accepting and respecting (plus teaching your children to accept and respect) the rules, the laws, the way of life, the culture of the place you want to live in. When you impose your presence on a country which didn't call you and however keeps you, integrating is the least you can comply with. Even more so, if you ask and obtain to become a citizen: a status which requires loyalty, reliability, trustworthiness, and possibly love for the Homeland you chose. Well: in Europe-Eurabia the other immigrants more or less integrate. Those who come from countries of Christian culture, I mean. From Russia, from Ukraine, from Bulgaria, from Hungary, from Slovenia. Even the questionable Chinese who defiantly lock themselves up in their mafiose enclaves, do somehow integrate. Muslims don't. Maybe here, in the United States, they do. In Europe, they don't. They don't even care to learn our languages. Glued to their mosques, to their Islamic Centers, to their hostility better yet their abhorrence and contempt for the West, they only obey the rules and the laws of Sharia. In return they impose on us their habits, their way of life. Food and poligamy included. In order to realize that Muslim immigrants have no intention to integrate with us infidel-dogs you only have to consider the Intifada which this Fall has burst in the region of Paris then all over France. Do you really believe what the media tells when it tells that those riots were exclusively dued to unemployment and poverty? Do you really believe that they had nothing to do with the war declared on us by Islam?

Those riots were and are another weapon of this war. They belonged and belong to the strategy of the Islamic invasion of Europe. A clever strategy indeed. Because, thanks to it, today's Islamic expansionism does not need the armies and the fleets of its dead Ottoman Empire. It only needs the hordes of immigrants who daily arrive by boat. A clever strategy also because it does not scare as their armies and their fleets and their scimitars used to. And because it requires time, patience, new generations to grow. Weren't the British kamikazes of July 7 immigrants of second and third generation? Aren't the French rioters of this Fall immigrants of second and third and even fourth generation? If I am wrong, tell me why among those rioters there were not poor and unemployed Chinese or Vietnamese or Philippinos or East Europe immigrants. Tell me why they were all Muslim Arabs, Muslim North-Africans. Tell me why in burning cars and buses and schools and pre-schools and post-offices and houses they yelled «Allah akbar, Allah akbar». Tell me why, when interviewed by journalists, they said «We are not French, we don't want to be French». Tell me why they acted in such a coordinated way, as if behind their deliriousness there were the mind of some Al Qaeda. Tell me also why, in Europe, Muslim immigrants materialize the 1974 Boumedienne's warning: «Soon we shall irrupt in the North emisphere. And not as friends. We shall irrupt to conquer. And we shall conquer by populating your territory with our children. It will be the womb of our women to give us victory».

Oh, yes. If we don't open our eyes and our minds, if we don't stop being so inert and suicidal, we Italians and French and Germans and British and Swedish and Danish and Dutch and so on, we'll soon reach the status that Comanches and Apaches and Cherokees and Navajos and Cheyennes and so on reached when we stole their continent. What is now America. Year 2016? Year 2100? In speaking of the Muslim future domination of Europe-Eurabia, some scholars already refer to us Europeans as to the «natives». To the «indigenous», to the «aborigines». At this pace we too shall end in the reservations.

Third and final point. I do not believe in the fraudolence of Moderate Islam. As I object in *Oriana Fallaci interviews herself* and *The Apocalypse*, what Moderate Islam?!? The one of the mendacious imams who once in a while blame a slaughter but soon after add a litany of «but», «however», «neverthless»?!? Is it enough not to handle explosives, not to cut heads off, or to chatter about peace-and-mercy, to be considered Moderate Muslims? Is it enough to wear double-breast suits instead of djellabahs, blue jeans instead of burkas or chadors, in order to be called the same way? And is it a moderate Muslim a Muslim who cudgels his wife or wives or kills his daughter if she falls in love with a Christian? Moderate Islam is another invention of ours. Another illusion fabricated by naïveté or Quislingness or misplaced realpolitik. Moderate Islam does not exist. And it does not exist because there is not such a thing as Good Islam or Bad Islam. There is Islam and that's all. And Islam is the Koran. Nothing but the Koran. And the Koran is the *Mein Kampf* of a religion which has always aimed to eliminate the others. A religion which identifies itself with politics, with governance. Which does not concede a nail's chip to free thought, to free choice. Which wants to substitute democracy with the mother of all totalitarianisms: theocracy. As I wrote in the essay *The Enemy we treat as a friend*, it is the Koran not my aunt Caroline which calls non-Muslims «infidel-dogs», meaning inferior beings, and which boasts that such dogs stink like monkeys or camels or pigs. It is the Koran not my aunt Caroline which asks to suppress them or at least subjugate them. It is the Koran not my aunt Caroline which humiliates women and preaches the Holy War, the Jihad. Ah! Read it over, that *Mein Kampf*. Whatever the version, you find out that all the evil which the sons of Allah commit against us and against themselves comes from that book. It is written in that book. And if saying so means vilifying Islam, Mr. Judge of my next trial, suit yourself. Do sentence me to all the years of prison you want. In prison I shall continue to repeat what I say now. I shall continue to shout: «Wake up, West, wake up! They have declared war on us, we are at war! And in war we must fight».

* * *

See? I could go on forever in sermonizing about these things. So I stop and I say: dear David, dear Daniel, dear Robert, dear comrades-in-arms with whom I share this award, dear friends of the Center for the Study of Popular Culture: indeed we fulfill a very difficult, a very grievous duty. The duty of speaking the Truth. And in speaking the Truth, giving voice to the voiceless. To the people who are misinformed or not informed at all, who sleep or don't think with their heads. And nevertheless people who when informed wake up, think with their heads and get to think what they did not know they were thinking.

We are not many, I admit. But we exist. We have always existed. We shall always exist. Under any fascism, any bolshevism, any McCartyism, any Islamism, any cancer of the brain, any cancer of the soul. And no matter the insults, the pillories, the persecutions, the mockeries, even the jails and the gulags and also the gallows which strike the body not the soul. Believe me: as bitter as it may be calling ourselves «outlaws-heretics-dissidents» in a society which defines itself as democratic and free, we really are the new heretics. The new outlaws. The new dissidents. So let me close this way: I am not as young and energetic as you are. I am not as healthy as I hope you are. To be blunt and brutal, I am hopelessly ill. I have reached what doctors call the End of the Road and I shall not last long. But the fact that you do what you do, that you will be here when I will be gone, helps me a lot to perform my duty against our enemies. To give them hell up to my last gasp of life. Better: as I said when I started talking, I don't caress the idea of imitating Annie Taylor. I am no fool. But if necessary, truly necessary, all right... I will take a deep breath, I will close my eyes, maybe I will make the Sign of Cross, (just in case and out of respect), then I will also jump over Niagara Falls.

Okay? Thanks for listening to me.

Oriana Fallaci

New York, November 28, 2005

Printed in Italy by
Nuovo Istituto Italiano d'Arti Grafiche - Bergamo
February 2006